P] Prejudice -- A Study Guide

By Francis Gilbert

This edition first published in 2015 by FGI publishing:
www.francisgilbert.co.uk;
fgipublishing.com
Copyright © 2015 Francis Gilbert
FGI Publishing, London UK, sir@francisgilbert.co.uk
ISBN-13: 978-1519145468

ISBN-10: 1519145462

Dedication
To my sister: Freya

Acknowledgments
First, huge thanks must go to my wife, Erica Wagner, for always supporting me with my writing and teaching. Second, I'm very grateful to all the students and teachers who have helped me write this book.

Also by Francis Gilbert:
I'm A Teacher, Get Me Out Of Here (2004)
Teacher On The Run (2005)
Yob Nation (2006)
Parent Power (2007)
Working The System: How To Get The Very State Education For Your Child (2011)
The Last Day Of Term (2012)
Gilbert's Study Guides on: *Frankenstein, Far From The Madding Crowd, The Hound of the Baskervilles , Pride and Prejudice, The Strange Case of Dr Jekyll and Mr Hyde, The Turn of the Screw, Wuthering Heights* (2013)
Dr Jekyll & Mr Hyde: The Study Guide Edition (2014)
Charlotte Brontë's Jane Eyre: The Study Guide Edition (2015)
Austen's Pride and Prejudice: The Study Guide Edition (2015)
Mary Shelley's Frankenstein: The Study Guide Edition (2015)
Brontë's Wuthering Heights: The Study Guide Edition (2015)

Contents

Part 1: Introduction

This study guide takes a different approach from most study guides. It does not simply tell you more about the story and characters, which isn't actually that useful. Instead, it attempts to show how the author's techniques and interests inform every single facet of this classic novel. Most study guides simply tell you *what* is going on, then tack on bits at the end which tell you *how* the author creates suspense and drama at certain points in the book, informing you a little about *why* the author might have done this.

This study guide starts with the *how* and the *why*, showing you right from the start *how* and *why* the author shaped the key elements of the book.

How to use this Study Guide

This study guide is deliberately interactive; it is full of questions, tasks and links to other sources of information. You will learn about *Pride and Prejudice* much more effectively if you have a go at the questions and tasks set, rather than just copying out notes.

Contexts

Definition:

The context of a book is both the *world* the book creates in the reader's mind (contexts of reading), and the *world* it came out from (contexts of writing).

Understanding Contexts

In order to fully appreciate a text, you need to appreciate the *contexts* in which it was written – known as its contexts of writing – and the *contexts* in which you read the book, or the contexts of reading.

This is potentially a huge area to explore because 'contexts' essentially means the 'worlds' from which the book has arisen. For the best books, these are many and various. The most obvious starting point is the writer's own life: it is worth thinking about how and why the events in a writer's life might have influenced his or her fiction. However, you do have to be careful not to assume too much. For example, many people think that the feisty central character of Elizabeth Bennet is a 'version' of Jane Austen herself but you must remember that Elizabeth Bennet is a character in her own right in the novel – a vital cog in the narrative wheel, a literary construct and not!

As a result, it is particularly fruitful to explore other contexts of writing. We can look at the broader world from which Jane Austen] arose (the melting pot of Georgian and Regency Britain), and consider carefully how, in her] writing, she both adopted and rejected the morals of her time. Other contexts might be the influence of the literary world that Jane Austen inhabited (what other authors were writing at the time), how religion shaped her views, and so on.

Just as important as the contexts of *writing* are the contexts of *reading*: how we read the novel today. Most of us have been heavily influenced by filmed versions of the novels before we read this most iconic of novels. Your own personal context is very important too. Depending upon your views about marriage, then you will read this novel in particular ways. Someone who believes that 'manners' and 'proper conduct' are not important in a marriage may well find this novel rather snobbish. In order for you to fully consider the contexts of reading rather than my telling you what to think, I have posed open-ended questions that seem to me to be important when considering this issue.

Questions

What do we mean by context? Why do you need to understand the idea of context in order to write well about *Pride and Prejudice*?

Contexts of Writing: Jane Austen's Life

There are two crucial points to remember when considering Jane Austen's life: she was from a large family which was on the fringes of becoming 'upper class' but was essentially 'middle class'. Perhaps the most important thing to bear in mind is that her social class was obsessed with 'ranking' people in a hierarchy because it hadn't quite 'made it'; it wasn't part of the aristocracy but wished to be and it turned its noses up at the 'common' middle class. Throughout the novel, we will see how this notion of 'ranking' people predominates; the gossip about the events in the novel – which occupies nearly half the text – is nearly always about the ways in which a person's behaviour betrays whether they are 'sincere' or 'vulgar' and who might be marrying who. This clearly was an obsession during Austen's own life and, in this sense, it is the 'gossipy' sections of the novel which are truest to her times, far more so than any of the romances that occupy the plots.

Born on 16 December 1775 at her father's rectory at Steventon in Hampshire, she was the seventh of eight children. Her father, George Austen, was a very respectable man indeed, having gained a scholarship to Oxford and then, after a stint as a schoolmaster, becoming a Fellow of his college. He trained to be a vicar and was offered a 'living' (in other words he was given a parish to be vicar of) at Steventon, Hamphire. He was very much an 'establishment' man; a Vicar who did not like the new fashion for 'evangelising' – preaching with real moral fervour – but preferred to be conservative, following the old traditions of the clergy, keeping his sermons moderate, following the customs of yesteryear. This is important because in all Austen's novels we see an inherent conservative; when Elizabeth Bennet 'moulds' Darcy it is not to make him a completely new man but simply to adapt his 'old' aristocratic ways to suit a more modern climate; the loss of Darcy's pride is not a revolution but a modification of what has gone before.

Jane had an older and only sister Cassandra; together they attended a rather miserable school in Southampton, before coming home because they fell ill with 'putrid fever' – schools in those days were breeding grounds for death and disease. They then attended a second school in Reading, which sounds rather better and more inspiring. However, they returned home in the mid 1780s to be educated by their older brothers James and Henry and their father. Their chief activities seem to have been playing the piano, drawing, writing letters, performing in amateur plays, walking in the countryside (but not far because it was considered dangerous), and going to periodic balls in the neighbourhood. Jane enjoyed dancing. However, they did not participate in the outdoor activities of their brothers who rode, hunted and went shooting. Being cooped up indoors much of the time, Jane developed the habit of writing.

George Austen died in 1805 and did not see his children flourish in the world. Three of his sons would ascend the hierarchy, reaching ranks of high distinction and Jane would become one of the most successful novelists of her day. However, in one very important way, neither daughter would fulfil a central ambition of the father; to be married. This was not because they were ugly. A cousin wrote of Jane and Cassandra being 'two of the prettiest girls in England.' Jane Austen's nephew wrote of his aunt when she was in her thirties: "In person she was very attractive; her figure was rather tall and slender, step light and firm, and her whole appearance expressive of health and animation.'

Austen began writing what is now termed 'juvenilia' in 1787 when she was twelve; this occupied most of her teenage years. They included short novels, sketches, batches of fictional letters, playlets and a history of England. By 1792, she was writing most serious work. In particular, she wrote *Evelyn*, which was a strange fable that was influenced by the Gothic novels of the day. Her first stab at tackling her central theme of the importance of 'candour' – being sincere in the way one expresses one's feelings – was the unfinished *Catherine*. By 1796, she had developed this theme more fully, and was working at a number of texts all of which would become important novels. However, they were initially given different names: *Elinor and Marianne* would become *Sense and Sensibility*, *Susan* would become *Northanger Abbey*, and *First Impressions* would become *Pride and Prejudice*.

Her life was quite eventual in the early 1800s: she seems to have had a brief romance with a man she met in Sidmouth but he died shortly afterwards, and she received a marriage proposal in 1802, which she accepted and then withdrew in the morning. Why did she not marry, given that her novels were all about this? The answer may lie in the reality of marriage at the time. Marriage was very time-consuming and dangerous for women; one in three women died in childbirth and the remainder that didn't had their whole lives occupied by children. Her brother's wife died shortly after marrying him, and her best friend, Mrs Lefroy, died in 1804. The truth is that Elizabeth Bennet would probably have died after marrying Darcy – and certainly would have not had time for any pursuits of her own if she had lived. Austen chose the path of the artist, giving up the chance to being a conventional woman of the time.

Her decision to pursue her writing career was, of course, absolutely the right one. In 1803, during the year when England renewed its war with France, she sold *Northanger Abbey* but it was returned in 1809 by the publishers. However, in 1811, *Sense and Sensibility* was published as being written by 'a Lady'. Two years later, *Pride and Prejudice* was published. She described it as her 'own darling child' and it garnered very favourable reviews. However, as with all of her novels during her lifetime, it was published anonymously and only a chosen, intellectual few knew of the books; it wasn't until after her death that she gained real fame and success.

She published *Mansfield Park* in 1814, and *Emma* in 1816, but by now she was becoming ill; she was suffering from Addison's Disease. She died on 18th July 1817. After she died *Northanger Abbey* and *Persuasion* were published. All of her novels followed a similarly comic format and explored the issue of marriage. It must be remembered that while novels had been written for nearly a century, it was still a relatively new form and regarded suspiciously by the establishment; rather like computer games are in our own age. Austen's chosen profession was not a 'respectable' one but it was the only one open to an intelligent middle-class woman; novelists were considered to be inferior to poets and writers who sought to inflame the minds of their readers with sensational plots and misleading ideas. This appears to be a view shared by Austen, who clearly viewed the form ambivalently; one of her novels, *Northanger Abbey*, is a parody of the Gothic novel and shows how a gullible female reader is seriously misled by the spooky novels she has read.

Jane Austen died well before her novels became the embodiment of 'respectability'.

Selected Reading & links on Jane Austen's Life

Claire Tomalin: *Jane Austen: A Life* (Penguin; 2003)]
More than any other biographer Tomalin finally nails the lie that Austen led the uneventful life of a scared, retiring spinster.
Maggie Lane: *Jane Austen's World: the Life and Times Of England's*

Most Popular Author (Carlton Books Ltd; 2005)

A good easily digested read about Austen's life, the world she lived in and the ways in which her work has lived on after her death.

The Pemberley website is excellent on the life, even though it looks pretty basic: **http://www.pemberley.com/janeinfo/janelife.html**

The whole Pemberley website should be explored too: **http://pemberley.com/**

The British Library website contains some excellent resources, including some very informative videos about Austen, her social context and her use of social realism in her novels. This page is an excellent starting point: **http://www.bl.uk/people/jane-austen**

Questions

What events, people and ideas in Austen's life and the wider society may have influenced the writing of *Pride and Prejudice*? Why is it important to consider her gender and social class?

Contexts of Reading

The contexts that we read Austen's novels now are very different from their original audience. A close examination of the novels reveals that they are very much products of their time; the obsession with marriage is not actually about love at all but about financial security and familial respectability. On the whole, we read the novels differently now because predominantly in the Western world marriage is largely about 'love' and not securing one's future.

Why is it then that Austen's novels have become even more popular than ever? This is largely because of the success of the films and TV series based on her work. While the filmed versions of *Pride and Prejudice* have much in common with the books; they differ in one crucial sense from the novel. At the heart of them, is 'romance'; Darcy is often represented as a 'Romantic' figure, a troubled, intense, poetic man who is inarticulate with his feelings. This is, inevitably, how we see Darcy now because this fits a convenient stereotype of romantic films and books; the difficult man who is, at heart, a sensitive soul. The films trace his development in this regard.

Yet, this is not how he is in the novel. He is not inarticulate about his feelings at all, and nor does Elizabeth want to 'draw out' his true self. There is actually very little that is romantic about Darcy at all in the novel; he is, in fact, an aristocratic man who is 'out of balance', he has too much pride in his social position, believing it to be the be-all and end-all. He develops as a character because Elizabeth guides him to this essentially rational realisation; he needs to modify his manners accordingly. Equally, Elizabeth is not 'prejudiced' against men or the upper classes – she does not suffer from the class envy that the films portray – she is simply prejudiced about Darcy because she jumps to false conclusions about his character on hearing Wickham's stories about him. When she realises that she has 'prejudged' Darcy before hearing his account, she learns the virtue of this rational approach.

To make films and TV shows that traced such rational responses and realisations would not entice a modern audience and so modern script-writers shape the characters to our expectations and not Austen's specifications. In this sense, we read the novel very differently now; we do not see it as a comic depiction of a philosophical realisation but as a dramatisation of the developing feelings of the characters.

Feelings have a very small but significant role in the novel; Elizabeth does confess that she loves Darcy at the end of the novel, but this is under duress. It is presented as an 'excessive' response, possibly an embarrassing but forgivable one. We though revel in this confession while Austen's readership may well have been uneasy about it.

We live in an age which Austen would have hated; an age where manners and notions of proper conduct have almost been entirely dispensed with in a 'codified' way. There are no explicit rules about how to behave which are accepted by society. Austen was not proposing sweeping away with notions of 'etiquette' – of good manners – but wished to modify the existing ones.

Useful links

The IMBD website contains the most comprehensive listing all of the Jane Austen related films:
http://www.imdb.com/name/nm0000807/
The Jane Austen Society of North America contains a useful webpage which discusses Austen and *Pride and Prejudice's* influence upon modern day culture:
http://jasna.org/film/pp.html
There are some useful reviews to be found on this commercial janeausten.co.uk website:
http://www.janeausten.co.uk/online-magazine/media-reviews/film-reviews/

Questions

Why is *Pride and Prejudice* such a popular novel today? Why have so many films/plays etc. been made of it?

Structure and Theme

The big question when examining *Pride and Prejudice's* structure is whether it is structurally flawed or not. Some critics have argued that Austen gets herself into all sorts of problems by resolving the central conflict of the novel far too soon. As the title suggests the novel focuses upon two central themes: 'pride' and 'prejudice'. The main male protagonist, Fitzwilliam Darcy, is afflicted by 'pride' – a curse of his aristocratic class which we see in its worst form in Lady Catherine de Bourgh -- while Elizabeth Bennet, of much humbler status, is afflicted by 'prejudice'. Again this 'prejudice' could be said to be a 'curse' of her social set – that of gentrified women who 'gossip. Elizabeth, in particular, is guilty of believing Wickham's lies about Darcy in which he stated that Darcy maliciously deprived him of his rightful inheritance because his pride.

The novel's initial title was 'First Impressions' because these two characters' first impressions lead to the central conflict of the novel; Darcy's pride leads to him resenting his feelings for Elizabeth, he knows that she is 'far beneath' him to marry and yet he feels compelled to marry her. Furthermore, his pride means that he stops his best friend Bingley from marrying Jane, Elizabeth's sister. Meanwhile Elizabeth's prejudice against Darcy, brought on by her first impressions of him and her believing Wickham's lies, lead her to rejecting the proposal. It the characters' 'first impressions' which are caused by their character flaws of pride and prejudice which lead them to clash. However, this important conflict is quickly resolved when Darcy sends Elizabeth a letter in which he shows real awareness that he was too full of pride to accept Elizabeth for who she truly was. He explains also that he felt Jane was indifferent to Bingley and that this was the reason why he discouraged Bingley from marrying her. Nevertheless, it is clear that he knows that his pride heavily influenced his advice. Perhaps even more importantly, Elizabeth learns that he had good reason to stop Wickham claiming a bequest left by Darcy's father because Wickham had attempted to seduce and elope with his fragile sister, Georgiana.

Elizabeth is mortified to read the letter and realises that she had been 'prejudiced' against Darcy; this is further confirmed when she stays with her aunt and uncle, the Gardiners, and visits Darcy's ancestral home, Pemberley, which embodies the truly good virtues of balance and harmony. Thus the central thematic conflict in the novel is resolved nearly half-way through the novel. Many critics have noted that this means Austen has to 'pad' out the rest of the novel with a great deal of rushing around in order to keep Darcy and Elizabeth apart until they are finally married a few hundred pages later. Other critics feel that Austen's genius lies in giving us a unique portrait of England during a time of huge social change and offering us a suspenseful, engaging plot.

You will need to think carefully about your attitude towards this central issue: does Austen resolve the conflict between Darcy and Elizabeth far too soon? Is the 'Lydia-Wickham' sub-plot sufficiently engaging to keep the momentum of the novel going? The majority of readers think so; Lydia's elopement with the 'wicked' Wickham gives the novel a scent of the 'sex scandal'; the pair are clearly living in 'sin' in London, neither married. Dashing to the rescue, Darcy 'buys out' Wickham by giving him a great deal of money to marry Lydia, he truly proves his heroic credentials and saves the whole family from gaining a ruinous reputation, much to Elizabeth's relief. Darcy then encourages Bingley to marry Jane. The issue of pride though raises its head when Lady Catherine de Bourgh, learning of Darcy's intention to marry Elizabeth rather than her own sickly daughter, tries to get Elizabeth to promise not to accept an offer of marriage from Darcy. For Lady Catherine, it is absurd that anyone from such a class as Elizabeth could marry an important aristocrat like Darcy. Elizabeth refuses to accede to her bullying, thus paving the way for her to accept Darcy's proposal when it comes.

Being ever mindful of the above comments which in some ways contradict what follows, we could break down the novel into the following structure:

Opening

Establishment of the main settings of Longbourn (the home of the Bennet family) and Netherfield (the residence of the Bingley family and Darcy for the first part of the novel)

Establishment of the main characters and their conflicts: Elizabeth's prejudice and Darcy's pride. A whole host of other important characters and their traits are dramatised, bringing vital comic colour to the novel. In particular, there is the Bennet family: Mr Bennet's dry, sarcastic humour and retreat from his 'female' family, Mrs Bennet's hysterical need to get her daughters married off at any cost, Jane Bennet's saintly patience and good humour, Lydia and Kitty giddy spirits and obsession with soldiers, Mary's good learning. While not notable characterisations, the Bingley family are very important in terms of the plot: Charles Bingley is a vapid young man who is Jane's intended, while his sister, Caroline Bingley, is jealous of Elizabeth's hold on Darcy.

Complications

Mr Collins, who is due to inherit Longbourn, proposes to Elizabeth and is rejected.

Mr Collins quickly proposes to Elizabeth's best friend, Charlotte Lucas, and is accepted.

Elizabeth learns from Wickham that Darcy stopped him from having a bequest he was due to get. Her prejudice against Darcy grows.

Bingley leaves Netherfield, disappointing Jane dreadfully.

Elizabeth visits the newly married Mr and Mrs Collins and meets Darcy at Rosings, Lady Catherine de Bourgh's. He proposes to her in a very high-handed fashion, saying it is "against his will" to marry her, but he can't help himself. Elizabeth rejects him, listing her complaints.

Crisis

Darcy sends a letter to Elizabeth explaining the truth about Wickham and admitting that he was too full of pride. She is mortified by her prejudice.

Lydia elopes with Wickham.

Climax

Apparently, Mr Gardiner ensures the marriage between Lydia and Wickham. A chance remark from Lydia reveals that it was actually Darcy who rescued the Bennet family reputation by paying Wickham to marry Lydia. Elizabeth totally changes her attitude towards Darcy.

Bingley becomes engaged to Jane.

Lady Catherine de Bourgh attempts to bully Elizabeth into rejecting any future proposals from Darcy.

Resolution

Elizabeth and Darcy marry.

Useful links to help you get to know the novel better

The BBC Bitesize website is probably the best of the "study guide" websites in that it contains information about the context, plot, characters and sample questions as well as videos and quizzes:

http://www.bbc.co.uk/schools/gcsebitesize/english_literature/proseprideprej/

Sparknotes also has detailed information and **a quiz** about the book:

http://www.sparknotes.com/lit/pride/

For me, the Gradesaver website contained the best chapter summaries; they were the clearest and most detailed:

http://www.gradesaver.com/pride-and-prejudice

The Wikipedia page at the time of writing contains a useful summary of the main characters and a very good visual organizer of the relationships between the characters.

Questions/tasks

Once you have read the book, ask yourself this question: to what extent is the novel a successful story? What are its exciting moments and why? Are there moments when the story feels less successful? Give reasons for your answers.

Compare one or two filmed versions with the novel; what events/characters/ideas do the film-makers use and what do they leave out, and why?

The Influence of Genre

To what extent was Austen influenced by the novels of her time?

Jane Austen was an avid reader and so it is hardly surprising that she was very influenced by the novels of her day. The novel was a relatively new form when she was writing and had only been in existence for fifty years or so; Austen was influenced by all the major writers who helped shaped its form. Perhaps the first of these was Daniel Defoe (1660-1731) who wrote much fiction including *Robinson Crusoe*, about a man stranded on a desert island, and *Moll Flanders*, about the life and times of a prostitute. Defoe was a journalist and used to writing 'fact' but used the same style of writing in his fiction to give it the feeling of truth. This was something that Austen imitated, bringing the same sort of realism to her novels as well; Austen's ability to describe people and places, their locations, their wealth, their families, was in part learnt from Defoe.

However, unlike Defoe, she was interested in describing her characters' feelings and thoughts. She no doubt learnt a great deal from the writer Samuel Richardson (1689-1761). His most famous novel was *Pamela*, which began life in 1739 as a series of letters that were written to show people have to write letters easily. From this Richardson gained the idea that he would write a series of 'morally instructive' letters that would educate the world about the dangers women faced from men. *Pamela* tells the story of the eponymous heroine who is a young, beautiful and talkative servant girl isolated from the parents who she writes to and in the power of Mr B, country gentleman. Mr B. falls in love with Pamela and tries everything to seduce before he, at the very end of the novel, marries her. The novel chiefly consists of Pamela's letters which describe her confused feelings for Mr B.: her horror at the thought of being raped by him, her desire for him, his desire for her, the various tricks he tries to play on her to get her to come to bed.

The novel was hugely influential and clearly shaped much of the form and narrative of *Pride and Prejudice*. Firstly, it was an 'epistolary' novel, that is a novel written as a series of letters: Austen, as well as using her ironic third person voice, uses letters to great effect in *Pride and Prejudice*, with some vital moments occurring in the letters that are written. Secondly, Richardson's theme is Austen's theme: the struggle for a good marriage. Thirdly, his emphasis upon describing the character's feelings is clearly a concern for Austen too. However, there are some major differences: Richardson was a strong moralist with a hard-hitting message which he liked to spell out very clearly: no sex before marriage. Austen was perhaps exactly of the same mind but she preferred to be more subtle in the way she conveyed her message. Hidden within the subplot of Lydia eloping with Wickham is the same message but it is not so explicitly stated.

Austen's unique 'ironic' tone was in part acquired from her reading of two other notable authors of the period: Jonathan Swift and Henry Fielding. Swift (1667-1745) wrote *Gulliver's Travels*, a story about Gulliver who travels to a variety of fantasy lands including Lilliput where everyone is one-twelfth the size of a human being and engaged in a ridiculously petty war with their neighbours. He also travels to other lands: a place of giants who treat humans as freak shows, and an island of mathematics and music where nothing they learn or do is practical. The tone is 'satirical' that is Swift is mocking with a purpose; making fun of the uselessness of certain people in Great Britain. In some of her portraits in *Pride and Prejudice* Austen does use satire; her protrayal of the grotesque Mr Collins and his slavish devotion to Lady Catherine de Bourgh, her characterisation of Mrs Bennet and her obsession with getting her daughters married off no matter what the cost, her portrait of the hideous Lady Catherine are all satirical because she is mocking for a very specific purpose, highlighting a central flaw in society's attitudes though her writing.

Perhaps from Henry Fielding (1707-1754) she learnt a gentler, less satirical and more ironical tone. Fielding said, "I describe not men, but manners; not an individual, but a species". His interest in manners is certainly Austen's. He was, above all, a satirist; his tone is more strongly mocking and condemning than Austen's but nevertheless the two writers share much in common beliefs. Both like to show how socially accepted ways of behaving often ignore real human needs and desires. Moreover, Austen clearly learnt a thing or two from Fielding's narratives which are action-packed; the second half of *Pride and Prejudice* is full of action of which Fielding would have been proud.

Lastly but not least, Austen was heavily influenced by a writer called Fanny Burney (1752-1840) whose novel *Evelina* was very important in establishing the genre. Burney's heroines were often far too good, beautiful and clever for their own good but the writer put them many fascinating situations. Her tone is perhaps closest to Austen's being above all 'ironic' rather than satirical. Burney's description of an eighteen-year-old girl's entrance into the society of London and other fashionable 'resorts' is both humorous and 'sentimental', attempting as it does to pull at the reader's heart strings. Much like Austen, Burney attempts to reveal the shallowness of much of fashionable society with her gentle, ironic tone. Of all the novels we have looked at, it is hers that perhaps had the most influence upon Austen in their subject matter and style of writing.

Useful links for Genre

The Shmoop website has a simple listing of the different genres which influenced the novel with some clear explanations:
http://www.shmoop.com/pride-and-prejudice/genre.html

The Wikipedia entry also is strong on this area:
https://en.wikipedia.org/wiki/Pride_and_Prejudice
The best thing to do is to read some other authors mentioned in this article and work out for yourself what influenced Austen.

Questions

How was Austen influenced by other writers and genres in the writing of *Pride and Prejudice*? Where did she learn her ironic tone from?

Critical Perspectives

To what extent was Jane Austen an intellectual novelist?

Many people like to think of Jane Austen as an isolated genius, writing her brilliant novels out in the remote villages of England, far away from the hustle and bustle of literary London, uninfluenced by the trends and fashions of the metropolis, an essentially 'unintellectual' writer who uses her intuition to write about people. This used to be the view of many critics until forty years ago, when researchers began to uncover documents that showed she was very well informed about many issues connected with her day and participated actively in many things.

Above all, Austen was influenced by two writers of very different sensibilities, writers in many ways embody the contradictions which she tries to resolve in her works: the polymath Samuel Johnson and the poet William Cowper. Firstly, she greatly admired Samuel Johnson (1709-84) who was the great man of letters of the eighteenth century; he edited and wrote much of what was to become the first 'proper' dictionary in the world and also penned some very influential novels and journalism. He was the wittiest, cleverest and most metropolitan writer of his day. He famously said: "Why, Sir, you find no man, at all intellectual, who is willing to leave London. No, Sir, when a man is tired of London, he is tired of life; for there is in London all that life can afford." Austen didn't have the luxury of being able to live in London even if she wanted to; she was born into a life of being a 'gentlewoman' of the country, the daughter of a provincial clergyman, and the option of living in London was not open to her unless she wanted to cause a scandal. However, this is not to say that she rejected living in a metaphorical 'London'; Johnson's comment in many ways is misinterpreted. He was not talking about the literal London but a 'metaphorical' place which embodied the qualities of hard work, striving, intellectual debate and challenge, literary production. In this sense, Austen created her own London of the mind and many of her most sympathetic characters are very Johnsonian in their outlook: they believe in striving and working their hardest. Darcy becomes the embodiment of the Johnsonian ideal at the end of *Pride and Prejudice* in the way he works so tirelessly to save the reputation of the Bennet family and win Elizabeth's affections. Arising from his profound faith in the value of hard work, Johnson felt that 'reason' perfected man; he was what we call a true 'Augustan' in this sense. This was a movement in the eighteenth century to put 'reason' and 'rationality' at the heart of the universe. Encouraged by Newton's discoveries in science, many intellectuals believed that the universe was, at heart, a profoundly rational place and that God was a rational omniscient being, and that reason was the highest peak of human achievement. Thus art, literature, painting, music and architecture which embodied the rational qualities of restraint, of symmetry, of balance, of harmony, of logic were celebrated above all others. In many ways, Austen was a devoted follower of this concept, although 'feelings' as opposed to logic to play an important part in her novels. However, it must be noted that the most important discoveries in *Pride and Prejudice* are intellectual ones, not emotional ones; Elizabeth learns to love Darcy once she has lost her 'irrational' prejudice, Darcy truly appreciates Elizabeth when he loses his unreasonable 'pride'..

Johnson wrote a great deal on the new form of the 'novel' – a craze which was sweeping through the educated classes of Europe. Realising that it was an emerging form, he set out to 'improve' it through criticism, which Austen clearly read with great interest. Among the many things he said perhaps the most important is Johnson's belief that the nearer fiction imitated life, the more it should seek teach subtle moral lessons. Austen herself had copied this advice when writing to her niece once. She said: "Wisdom is better than Wit, and in hte long run will certainly have the laugh on her side". We can clearly see Austen shaping *Pride and Prejudice* along Johnsonian principles with the way the author engineers the narrative so that the two main characters clearly learn important moral lessons about how to live their lives without pride and prejudice.

Austen was very influenced by the poet, William Cowper (1731-1800), too though. Cowper was Johnson's opposite: a quiet, reclusive poet who shunned the city and made a virtue of this in his poetry. He famously wrote:

"God made the country, and man made the town:
What wonder that health and virtue, gifts
That can make sweet the bitter draught
That life holds out to all, should most abound
And least be threatened in the fields and groves?"

Cowper believed that the countryside naturally encouraged 'health' and 'virtue'. Many thinkers and scientists believed that nature embodied God's great 'rational' design; this was before Darwin arrived at his theory of evolution and therefore many intellectuals believed that nature was directly shaped and moulded by God to bring harmony and order to the human mind, fostering the virtues of rationality, hard work, balance. *The Task* is the longest and most famous of Cowper's poems and it clearly influenced

Austen a great deal; it seeks to encourage men to 'retire' from the metropolitan life and suggests that the country life far from being usless, idle and empty is meaningful because it encourages wisdom. It suggests that being 'humble' and warmth of heart is the best way of being. Both virtues that Austen subtly argues for in *Pride and Prejudice*. In many ways, Austen's belief in Cowper's advocacy for feelings is in contradiction to her adherence to Johnson belief in 'reason'. Much of the tension generated in her books is caused by this contradiction between 'sentiment' or feeling and 'reason'. For example, Darcy is most vivid as a character when he is tormented by his intellectual appraisal of Elizabeth – he assesses her to be beneath him – and his actual feelings for her.

All the evidence suggests that Austen thought very carefully about the ideas that infuse her books. She was no simple moralist who was offering the reader a simplistic message but nevertheless did see that novels could be 'morally instructive', promoting proper modes of behaviour. In this sense, she was and remains a powerful 'moral philosopher'.

Selected Reading & Links for literary criticism

Christopher Gillie: *A Preface to Austen – revised edition* (Longman; 1985)

The Preface series remain models of excellence. This one is no exceptional; Gillie is excellent at highlighting the ways in which Austen was influenced by the period she lived in and provides generous quotation from other authors so that the reader can really see how Austen was influenced by writers of her day.

Deirdre Le Fay: *Jane Austen: the World Of Her Novels* (Frances Lincoln; 2003)

A must-have book for anyone interested in the background to the novels as well as a pretty good 'crib' on the novels too: replete with clear summaries of the novels and explanations of the sort of world they arose from.

Robert Morrison (editor): *Pride and Prejudice – A Sourcebook* (Routledge; 2005)

The definitive critical guide which contains most of what you will need to know about the novel.

The British Library contains some of the best resources on the web for Jane Austen, with top literary critics commenting on her work in print and on video. The following link is a good starting point, but I strongly advise you to look at all the resources on the BL website for Austen:

http://www.bl.uk/romantics-and-victorians/articles/jane-austens-social-realism-and-the-novel

The Signet Classics Teacher's Guide to Pride and Prejudice contains a number of excellent ideas for teachers and students, with essay questions, great activities and useful vocabulary etc:

http://www.penguin.com/static/pdf/teachersguides/PridePrej udice.pdf

Questions

What differing views do literary critics have of the novel? Which critics do you most agree with and why? Which ones do you agree with the least and why?

Part 2: Extracts & Questions

How to read and study the novel

What follows are selected extracts from *Pride and Prejudice* interspersed with commentaries and questions on the text. I have deliberately provided a variety of different question types at the ends of chapters; I have started with "simple" comprehension questions and then moved onto more analytical and creative questions, which require you to understand the plot. I have deliberately tailored the comprehension questions (not the GCSE/A Level style questions or creative ones) to address the points made on the **Gradesaver chapter summaries** website so that you can easily look up the answers to these questions, which are checking you know the story, characters and settings.

Remember if you are uncertain about the plot, you can also refer to the websites listed in the section **'Useful weblinks for the story'**. These websites are good at helping you understand the plot but they won't help you get the higher marks because you really need to think for yourself if you are going to get the top grades. Throughout the book, **you should keep a vocabulary list**, writing down the difficult words and learning their meanings/spellings, and possibly using the vocabulary in your own writing. **The Signet Classics Teacher's Guide to Pride and Prejudice** contains a useful vocabulary list of the most important difficult works (p. 22) if you are struggling, good summaries and a useful character list. It's aimed at teachers, but students could easily use it and it's free! Reading this book is a great opportunity to learn new, exciting words. Don't be put off by the language, embrace it, love it! You will become much better educated when you learn the vocabulary. This is why reading pre-20th century writing is so useful: it makes you more intelligent because you widen your vocabulary and ability to understand difficult passages.

You could while reading the book put all your answers, notes, creative responses together into a *Pride and Prejudice* file or learning journal. You could be creative with this file: draw scenes of the important incidents; include spider-diagrams/visual organisers of the people Elizabeth encounters and the situations she finds herself in; storyboards of the key scenes; copies of articles/literary criticism which you have annotated; creative pieces etc.

Helpful vocabulary to learn before you start reading

As I have already said, keeping a vocabulary book is extremely important while reading this book. However, there are some words, I would strongly advise you looking up the meanings of and learning their spellings/meanings before reading. These words are the ones highlighted on p. 22 of the **Signet Teacher's Guide to Pride and Prejudice**; this study guide helpfully associates particular characters with these words. This is very useful to know; since this guide is free on the internet, I strongly advise you looking at this page. The words are: fastidious, ductility, supercilious, impertinent, pedantic, insipidity, indolent, laconic, affability, condescension, obsequiousness, pompous, diffidence, candid, ostentation, duplicity, officious. They are all words in common use today so it is strongly recommended you learn them and use them.

You can find a useful vocabulary list of difficult words from *Pride and Prejudice* here:

http://www.vocabulary.com/lists/228620#view=notes

Cliffnotes has a full (and long!) glossary of difficult words from the book here:

http://www.cliffsnotes.com/literature/p/pride-and-prejudice/study-help/full-glossary-for-pride-and-prejudice

Rather than trying to learn these words immediately, I would refer to this glossary as you read the book, adding to your vocabulary list as you read.

You can find a list of the difficult words as they appear in the novel here:

https://myvocabulary.com/word-list/novels/pride-and-prejudice-vocabulary/

There is a rather cool set of flashcards for the novel to be found here, you need to sign in to get access to the facility:

https://quizlet.com/167646/english-vocabulary-pride-and-prejudice-flash-cards/

There is another vocabulary quiz to be found here, aimed at US students taking SATS, but it is quite useful:

http://www.verbalworkout.com/b/b1017.htm

Chapter 1

Extract

It is a truth universally acknowledged, that a single man in possession of a good fortune, must be in want of a wife.

However little known the feelings or views of such a man may be on his first entering a neighbourhood, this truth is so well fixed in the minds of the surrounding families, that he is considered the rightful property of some one or other of their daughters.

Analysis: The most famous opening sentence of any novel stands alone, given its own paragraph, glittering magnificently with a whole host of possible meanings and interpretations. Above all, Austen is being ironic, using the third person voice to echo the concerns of a society obsessed with 'marrying well'. The adverb 'universally' is both comic and mysterious, prompting all sorts of inquiries; is this truth really 'universally' known? If so, what constitutes the 'universe' in this novel? The adverb is ironically comic because, of course, this truth is not 'universally acknowledged' at all, and therefore is not a 'truth' at all but a 'supposition' or 'guess' promoted by people who want to believe it is true i.e. self-interested people such as parents who wish to marry off their daughters to rich men. The noun phrase 'good fortune' is important because it suggests that not only that the man in question has great wealth but it slyly connotes the idea that he is lucky; in other words, a rich, 'lucky' man must need a wife. As with many of Austen's most memorable sentences, the rhythm of the sentence is very pleasing on the ear, rolling off the tongue fluently until it comes to a heavy stop on the monosyllable of 'wife'. Notice Austen's play on the word 'want' which contains both its modern and archaic meaning; 'want' suggests that man must desire a wife and also be 'lacking' a wife. Moreover, a wife is a vital addition for a rich man, a 'possession'.

Discussion point What are our attitudes towards wealthy, single men now? Do we believe that they must, above all, need a wife? Why do you think that it was so important in Austen's time for men to have wives? Why is it important now for men to have a wife? Why is it important to be married?

Extract

"Mr. Bennet, how *can* you abuse your own children in such a way? You take delight in vexing me. You have no compassion for my poor nerves."

"You mistake me, my dear. I have a high respect for your nerves. They are my old friends. I have heard you mention them with consideration these last twenty years at least."

"Ah, you do not know what I suffer."

"But I hope you will get over it, and live to see many young men of four thousand a year come into the neighbourhood."

"It will be no use to us, if twenty such should come, since you will not visit them."

"Depend upon it, my dear, that when there are twenty, I will visit them all."

Mr. Bennet was so odd a mixture of quick parts, sarcastic humour, reserve, and caprice, that the experience of three-and-twenty years had been insufficient to make his wife understand his character. *Her* mind was less difficult to develop. She was a woman of mean understanding, little information, and uncertain temper. When she was discontented, she fancied herself nervous. The business of her life was to get her daughters married; its solace was visiting and news.

Analysis: Notice how quickly Austen moves from the very general to the specific. Having provided us with this huge, sweeping generalisation about rich, single men, she now focuses immediately upon the Bennet household, allowing us to eavesdrop upon a personal conversation between a husband and wife. This is a technique she uses throughout all her work; providing an ironic generalisation and then homing in immediately upon a very specific scene. It is apparent that her portrait of Mrs Bennet is immediately satirical; her presentation of her is highly comical. Mrs Bennet is presented as being slightly hysterical, vulgar and nakedly materialistic, clearly happy to use her daughters as a means of social climbing. The juxtaposition of these two sentences is interesting: "*A single man of large fortune; four or five thousand a-year. What a fine thing for our girls and therefore you must visit him as soon as he comes!*" It is clear that the only reason why it would be a fine thing for her daughters to visit Bingley is because he has '*four or five thousand a year*'. Mr Bennet forms a sharp contrast with Mrs Bennet; where she is brash and out-spoken, he is quiet and reserved, where she is obviously vulgar and money-grabbing, he is cultured and, on the surface, little interested in monetary matters. His comments are 'sarcastic': "*I have a high respect for your nerves. They are my old friends. I have heard you mention them with consideration these twenty years at least.*" His personification of her nerves gives the reader a powerful sense that his life has been dominated by her moods or 'uncertain temper' as Austen terms it.

Discussion point Why does Austen use dialogue in this chapter? What do you think of her presentation of Mr and Mrs Bennet? Do characters like Mr and Mrs Bennet still exist?

Questions

How many daughters do Mr and Mrs Bennet have?

Why is Mrs Bennet keen to see them married? What does she hope their new neighbour Mr Bingley might do? Why is Mr Bingley so appealing to

Mrs Bennet?

What does Mrs Bennet wish that her husband might do? What is Mr Bennet's response?

Why are Jane and Lydia Mrs Bennet's favourite daughters?

You can find the answers for the above questions embedded in the chapter summaries on the **Gradesaver website here**.

GCSE/A Level style question: How does Austen create comedy in this first chapter?

Creative response: Write Elizabeth's diary for this chapter, exploring her thoughts about the new arrivals in the area and her mother.

Chapter 2

Extract

"I am sick of Mr. Bingley," cried his wife.

"I am sorry to hear *that*; but why did not you tell me that before? If I had known as much this morning I certainly would not have called on him. It is very unlucky; but as I have actually paid the visit, we cannot escape the acquaintance now."

The astonishment of the ladies was just what he wished; that of Mrs. Bennet perhaps surpassing the rest; though, when the first tumult of joy was over, she began to declare that it was what she had expected all the while.

Analysis: Throughout the story, Austen builds suspense by having characters gossip about an absent character who they desire. Much of the first section of the novel is occupied with various people talking about Bingley, he of the 'good fortune', and speculating upon his wishes. Austen further develops her suspense by leading the reader to believe that it is unlikely that the 'gossipers' will meet the person they are gossiping about soon – if indeed at all – thus creating a leisurely comic tone to the narrative; the reader draws pleasure not in the 'events' of the novel, but delights in the different perceptions of the gossipers. Then, once the reader is resigned to reading a novel about people discussing other people in drawing rooms with nothing actually happening, something does indeed happen. This technique is illustrated here: we expect to read a great deal more dialogue about Bingley, but not to encounter him. However, the father's sly, ironic aside indicating that he has called on Bingley propels the story forward, making us realise that this is a novel of 'events' as well as 'discussion'.

Discussion point In what ways does Austen make the 'gossip' interesting?

Questions

Who does Mr Bennet visit? What is the name of this place? Why did he only tell Mrs Bennet a few days after his visit?

Why and how does Mr Bennet make his wife and daughters angry?

You can find the answers for the above questions embedded in the chapter summaries on the **Gradesaver website here**.

GCSE style question: How does Austen present Mr and Mrs Bennet's marriage in these first two chapters?

Creative response: write Mr Bennet or Mrs Bennet's diary for this chapter, outlining their thoughts and feelings for each other.

Chapter 3

Extract

Elizabeth Bennet had been obliged, by the scarcity of gentlemen, to sit down for two dances; and during part of that time, Mr. Darcy had been standing near enough for her to hear a conversation between him and Mr. Bingley, who came from the dance for a few minutes, to press his friend to join it.

"Come, Darcy," said he, "I must have you dance. I hate to see you standing about by yourself in this stupid manner. You had much better dance."

"I certainly shall not. You know how I detest it, unless I am particularly acquainted with my partner. At such an assembly as this it would be insupportable. Your sisters are engaged, and there is not another woman in the room whom it would not be a punishment to me to stand up with."

"I would not be so fastidious as you are," cried Mr. Bingley, "for a kingdom! Upon my honour, I never met with so many pleasant girls in my life as I have this evening; and there are several of them you see uncommonly pretty."

"*You* are dancing with the only handsome girl in the room," said Mr. Darcy, looking at the eldest Miss Bennet.

> Analysis: The first appearance of Mr Darcy is notable because he is clearly a marked contrast to his friend Bingley. As we have seen with Mr and Mrs Bennet, Austen's literary technique is to create 'pairs' of characters who are intimately bound to each other, either by familial relationship or friendship, and then point out their different qualities. Her language is extremely subtle but telling. Bingley is described as 'good-looking' whereas Darcy is 'handsome', thus telling the reader that Darcy is the more attractive of the two. Bingley is 'gentlemanlike' but Darcy is 'fine'; once again the distinction is important. 'Fine' is a simple sounding adjective but carries with it a great many different connotations: it means Darcy, like his sisters, is 'upper class' and 'extremely well-mannered' but also there are hints

of aloofness and snobbishness. This quality is further enhanced by the noun phrase of 'noble mien'; once again this sense that Darcy is aristocratic and rarefied in his manners is suggested. Most significantly, Austen rounds off this particular sentence with the news that he has 'ten thousand a year'. As we saw with Bingley's 'four or five thousand a year', it is the money which is the most important in this particular company. Darcy is moving amongst a lower class of person than he is used to and they, having either little money like the Bennets or having derived their money from trade, have a salacious interest in finance and men's incomes. The narrative voice reflects the interests of this community in an ironic fashion.

Austen then subtly begins to speak for the whole of this socially aspiring community when she says that 'he was discovered to be proud'. The adjective 'proud' and its noun form 'pride' dominate the novel; Austen carefully shapes the novel so that Darcy learns to lose his 'pride' through his encounters with Elizabeth. The word 'proud' is similar to 'fine' in its effects; it suggests a snobbishness of approach. It is more judgemental though, implicitly condemning Darcy for deeming himself to be too good for the company he is with. Austen in this sense is a democrat; she believes that no person has the right to sneer and that this is downright poor manners. Notice though, it is difficult to unpick the narrative voice from the voice of the community because of Austen's ironic voice; it is only when we see him reject Elizabeth as a dancing partner that we realise that the author ultimately agrees that Darcy is too proud.

Discussion point: Why does Austen present Darcy so unsympathetically at this point in the novel?

Extract

"Oh! She is the most beautiful creature I ever beheld! But there is one of her sisters sitting down just behind you, who is very pretty, and I dare say very agreeable. Do let me ask my partner to introduce you."

"Which do you mean?" and turning round he looked for a moment at Elizabeth, till catching her eye, he withdrew his own and coldly said: "She is tolerable, but not handsome enough to tempt *me*; I am in no humour at present to give consequence to young ladies who are slighted by other men. You had better return to your partner and enjoy her smiles, for you are wasting your time with me."

Analysis: Darcy epithet 'tolerable' which describes Elizabeth is fascinating because while it condemns her as being rather unexceptional, it also acknowledges that she is good looking but not in a way that is striking. It is a word which will haunt Elizabeth later on.

Discussion point Do we still judge and measure women by
their looks nowadays?

Questions

Who visits the house? Do the daughters see him or not?

Where does Mrs Bennet get her information about Bingley?

Once Mrs Bennet has heard about Bingley, what does she believe she can
engineer?

Who does Mrs Bennet invite to dinner? What is his response?

When do the Bennet sisters meet Bingley? Who else do they meet?

What is the Bennet sisters' opinion of Mr Darcy?

Who refuses to dance with Elizabeth and why? What is Elizabeth's
response?

What do the Bennet sisters think of Bingley?

What is Mr Bennet's reaction when Mrs Bennet tries to explain what
happened at the ball?

You can find the answers for the above questions embedded in the
chapter summaries on the **Gradesaver website here**.

GCSE style question: how does Austen make the ball such an exciting and
suspenseful occasion?

Creative response: write Elizabeth's diary for this chapter, outlining her
thoughts and feelings about Darcy and the ball.

Chapter 4

Extract

"*You* began the evening well, Charlotte," said Mrs. Bennet with civil self-
command to Miss Lucas. "*You* were Mr. Bingley's first choice."

"Yes; but he seemed to like his second better."

"Oh! you mean Jane, I suppose, because he danced with her twice. To be
sure that *did* seem as if he admired her—indeed I rather believe he *did*—I
heard something about it—but I hardly know what—something about Mr.
Robinson."

"Perhaps you mean what I overheard between him and Mr. Robinson;
did not I mention it to you? Mr. Robinson's asking him how he liked our
Meryton assemblies, and whether he did not think there were a great many
pretty women in the room, and *which* he thought the prettiest? and his
answering immediately to the last question: 'Oh! the eldest Miss Bennet,
beyond a doubt; there cannot be two opinions on that point.'"

"Upon my word! Well, that is very decided indeed—that does seem as if—
but, however, it may all come to nothing, you know."

"*My* overhearings were more to the purpose than *yours*, Eliza," said
Charlotte. "Mr. Darcy is not so well worth listening to as his friend, is he?—
poor Eliza!—to be only just *tolerable*."

Analysis: As we saw in the opening chapters, much of the pleasure of the novel lies in reading the dialogue which reflects upon the central 'events', affording the reader the chance to live the ball once again through the eyes of the different characters. Thus the reader enriches his understanding of the various psychological and social hierarchies, placing the characters in a definite pecking order. Thus at this point because Charlotte has been asked by Bingley to dance first, she deserves to advance up the 'hierarchy' of marriageable women. However, Jane is placed above her because Bingley asked her to dance twice; Mrs Bennet's transparently insincere modesty about Jane 'Oh! you mean, Jane,' can't hide her pride in the fact that Jane is obviously at the top of the hierarchy. Because she is the mother of such a desired girl, she believes this places her above Lady Lucas within the terms of reference of this conversation, scoring a major social triumph over someone who is manifestly her social superior because she is a 'Lady'. However, we realise that she is not a real 'Lady' because her husband was not born into the aristocracy but was 'formerly in trade', which means that he is basically of 'common' stock. In such a way, Austen begins to weave a complex picture of the 'pecking order'; amongst this Hampshire community, it is 'fluid'; everyone is on the 'make', trying to better themselves through marriage, trade and by associating with the right people. The tension in the novel is generated because we already care about Jane and Elizabeth; we want them to triumph above the dull Charlotte Lucas and the waspish Bingley sisters. But we realise that they have every disadvantage bar their good looks and Eliza's intelligence: they are saddled with an embarrassing mother, a largely absent father, a relatively lowly social position and no money or fortune attached to them. Austen gives them these social positions in order to generate sympathy and make the odds against them succeeding appear quite significant.

Discussion point The social hierarchy that Austen dramatises here is both complex and subtle. In what ways is it complex and subtle?

Questions

What do we learn about the Lucas family at the beginning of the chapter?

What do Charlotte and Mrs Lucas say about the ball during their visit to Longbourn? What do they criticize Darcy for?

What does Mary say about pride and vanity?

You can find the answers for the above questions embedded in the chapter summaries on the **Gradesaver website here**.

GCSE style question: how does Austen explore the themes of pride and vanity in these opening chapters?

Creative response: write Mary's diary for the opening chapters of the novel.

Chapter 5

Extract

Mr. Bingley inherited property to the amount of nearly a hundred thousand pounds from his father, who had intended to purchase an estate, but did not live to do it. Mr. Bingley intended it likewise, and sometimes made choice of his county; but as he was now provided with a good house and the liberty of a manor, it was doubtful to many of those who best knew the easiness of his temper, whether he might not spend the remainder of his days at Netherfield, and leave the next generation to purchase.

His sisters were anxious for his having an estate of his own; but, though he was now only established as a tenant, Miss Bingley was by no means unwilling to preside at his table—nor was Mrs. Hurst, who had married a man of more fashion than fortune, less disposed to consider his house as her home when it suited her. Mr. Bingley had not been of age two years, when he was tempted by an accidental recommendation to look at Netherfield House. He did look at it, and into it for half-an-hour—was pleased with the situation and the principal rooms, satisfied with what the owner said in its praise, and took it immediately.

Between him and Darcy there was a very steady friendship, in spite of great opposition of character. Bingley was endeared to Darcy by the easiness, openness, and ductility of his temper, though no disposition could offer a greater contrast to his own, and though with his own he never appeared dissatisfied. On the strength of Darcy's regard, Bingley had the firmest reliance, and of his judgement the highest opinion. In understanding, Darcy was the superior. Bingley was by no means deficient, but Darcy was clever. He was at the same time haughty, reserved, and fastidious, and his manners, though well-bred, were not inviting. In that respect his friend had greatly the advantage. Bingley was sure of being liked wherever he appeared, Darcy was continually giving offense.

Analysis: Once again, we see Austen using the technique of making Bingley and Darcy 'binary opposites', that is she is constantly comparing and contrasting them. The sentence which is most telling is: *"Bingley was endeared to Darcy by the easiness, openness, and ductility of his temper, though no disposition could offer a greater contrast to his own."* Thus Austen suggests implicitly that Darcy is not 'easy' or 'open' or ductile in temperament – in other words, he is possibly bad-tempered. We also pick up some similarities with Elizabeth here: he is 'clever' like she is, and, though in a different fashion to the out-spoken Elizabeth, he is 'continually giving offence'. Thus Austen generates much suspense in her characterisation, painting a relatively complex portrait of a difficult, conflicted man who is finding it hard to find his natural company. In his aloofness there is a suggestion of 'loneliness'; although Austen does not develop this romantic quality much in the novel – certainly not as much as the numerous film and TV versions do – we can begin to see Darcy as a fore-runner to troubled, romantic protagonists such as Rochester in *Jane Eyre*.

Discussion point: How does Austen generate suspense in her presentation of Darcy here?

Questions

What does Jane admit she feels about Bingley when she is alone with Elizabeth?

What advice does Elizabeth give to her?

What do we learn about the wealth of Darcy and Bingley? What do we learn about their characters?

What do Bingley and Darcy think about the Meryton ball? Why is Darcy not that impressed with Jane? What do the Bingley sisters think of her?

You can find the answers for the above questions embedded in the chapter summaries on the **Gradesaver website here**.

GCSE style question: how does Austen portray the relationships between Jane and Elizabeth?

Creative response: write Elizabeth's diary for this chapter, recording her thoughts and feelings about Jane.

Chapter 6

Extract

Occupied in observing Mr. Bingley's attentions to her sister, Elizabeth was far from suspecting that she was herself becoming an object of some interest in the eyes of his friend. Mr. Darcy had at first scarcely allowed her to be pretty; he had looked at her without admiration at the ball; and when they next met, he looked at her only to criticise. But no sooner had he made it clear to himself and his friends that she hardly had a good feature in her face, than he began to find it was rendered uncommonly intelligent by the beautiful expression of her dark eyes. To this discovery succeeded some others equally mortifying. Though he had detected with a critical eye more than one failure of perfect symmetry in her form, he was forced to acknowledge her figure to be light and pleasing; and in spite of his asserting that her manners were not those of the fashionable world, he was caught by their easy playfulness. Of this she was perfectly unaware; to her he was only the man who made himself agreeable nowhere, and who had not thought her handsome enough to dance with.

Analysis: Notice here the fluidity and grace of Austen's prose style and the effortless way her third person narrative affords her the chance to switch perspective. This section starts off with seeing the world through Elizabeth's eyes, her lack of awareness that she was the object of desire. Then it moves into examining his changing perceptions of Elizabeth, talking about the conversations he had been having with his friends where he is derogatory about Elizabeth. This sentence is marvellous because of its juxtaposition of opposites; it talks of Darcy saying 'she had hardly a good feature in her face' but follows this statement with 'he began to find it was rendered uncommonly intelligent by the beautiful expression of her dark eyes'. As with so many of Austen's great sentences, it is the way that she ends them that makes them so perfect; the 'dark eyes' embody both her beauty and her intelligence. We are now entering the innermost heart of Darcy's desires and thought-processes. Later, in her most complex novel Emma, Austen will develop her ability to enter a major character's thought processes, but here she immediately pulls away, returning back to Elizabeth's lack of awareness.

Discussion point How successful is Austen's use of the third person here?

Questions

Who visits Longbourn several times and why? What differing views do Jane and Elizabeth have about their visitors?

What advice does Charlotte Lucas give Elizabeth about how Jane should behave with Bingley? What is Elizabeth's response?

What attracts Darcy to Elizabeth?

At dinner, who does Darcy spy upon and why?

What is Elizabeth's response when Sir William Lucas begs her to dance with Darcy?

Who does Darcy tell about his admiration for Elizabeth and what is her response? Why does Darcy not mock Elizabeth even though he is being encouraged to?

You can find the answers for the above questions embedded in the chapter summaries on the **Gradesaver website here**.

GCSE style question: how does Austen develop the characters of Darcy and Elizabeth in this chapter?

Creative response: write Darcy's diary for this chapter.

Chapter 7

Extract

Mr. Bennet's property consisted almost entirely in an estate of two thousand a year, which, unfortunately for his daughters, was entailed, in default of heirs male, on a distant relation; and their mother's fortune, though ample for her situation in life, could but ill supply the deficiency of his. Her father had been an attorney in Meryton, and had left her four thousand pounds.

Analysis: Austen further ratchets up the suspense by revealing to us that the Bennet family's fortunes are far from secure, hanging on the slender thread of the father living a very long life or the girls marrying well. Thus she shows us that far from being a frivolous occupation, the business of marriage is very much that; a business. It is the only means that the girls have of securing a stable future. In this sense, for all her presentation of Mrs Bennet as being a ridiculous person in being so obsessed with marrying off her daughters, we gain a deeper sense here that she has a point.

Discussion point: How have our perceptions of marriage changed since the novel was first written?

Extract

Their visits to Mrs. Phillips were now productive of the most interesting intelligence. Every day added something to their knowledge of the officers' names and connections. Their lodgings were not long a secret, and at length they began to know the officers themselves. Mr. Phillips visited them all, and this opened to his nieces a store of felicity unknown before. They could talk of nothing but officers; and Mr. Bingley's large fortune, the mention of which gave animation to their mother, was worthless in their eyes when opposed to the regimentals of an ensign.

After listening one morning to their effusions on this subject, Mr. Bennet coolly observed:

"From all that I can collect by your manner of talking, you must be two of the silliest girls in the country. I have suspected it some time, but I am now convinced."

Analysis: The arrival of the officers produces a marked shift in tone in the novel. Shortly, the military will dominate the thoughts of the characters. Many critics have noted that Austen does not dwell at all upon the actual purpose of the military being posted throughout the country; from the time the book was first conceived and published, from the 1790s to the 1810s, England became increasingly a military state, fearing that the French would invade. No mention of this national panic is slipped into the novel. Instead, it is the romantic qualities of the officers that is focussed upon. This was not because Austen was ignorant of the army's purposes, but because she is much more interested in the destabilising effect that they have upon the residents' hearts and minds rather than their actual military purposes. Notice though how Mr Bennet is impatient with the frivolous gossip about the soldiers.

Discussion point What are our attitudes towards soldiers now? Are they perceived as men deserving of romantic attention?

What is Austen's purpose in introducing them at this point in the novel?

Extract

"Dining out," said Mrs. Bennet, "that is very unlucky."

"Can I have the carriage?" said Jane.

"No, my dear, you had better go on horseback, because it seems likely to rain; and then you must stay all night."

"That would be a good scheme," said Elizabeth, "if you were sure that they would not offer to send her home."

"Oh! but the gentlemen will have Mr. Bingley's chaise to go to Meryton, and the Hursts have no horses to theirs."

"I had much rather go in the coach."

"But, my dear, your father cannot spare the horses, I am sure. They are wanted in the farm, Mr. Bennet, are they not?"

"They are wanted in the farm much oftener than I can get them."

"But if you have got them to-day," said Elizabeth, "my mother's purpose will be answered."

She did at last extort from her father an acknowledgment that the horses were engaged. Jane was therefore obliged to go on horseback, and her mother attended her to the door with many cheerful prognostics of a bad day. Her hopes were answered; Jane had not been gone long before it rained hard. Her sisters were uneasy for her, but her mother was delighted. The rain continued the whole evening without intermission; Jane certainly could not come back.

"This was a lucky idea of mine, indeed!" said Mrs. Bennet more than once, as if the credit of making it rain were all her own.

Analysis: The presentation of Mrs Bennet is fascinating here; she is, as ever, presented in an ironic light, appearing cheerfully heartless as she sends Jane off on horseback into a hoped-for 'bad day'. Her delusions of grandeur border on the insane, believing that the 'credit of making it rain were all her own.' A strange thing happens here though because the reader, for all his laughter at Mrs Bennet's unreasonable behaviour, hopes that she is right; we want Jane to stay at Netherfield. We drawn into a troubling collusion with Mrs Bennet here.

Discussion point What do you think of the presentation of Mrs Bennet here?

Extract

She was shown into the breakfast-parlour, where all but Jane were assembled, and where her appearance created a great deal of surprise. That she should have walked three miles so early in the day, in such dirty weather, and by herself, was almost incredible to Mrs. Hurst and Miss Bingley; and Elizabeth was convinced that they held her in contempt for it. She was received, however, very politely by them; and in their brother's manners there was something better than politeness; there was good humour and kindness. Mr. Darcy said very little, and Mr. Hurst nothing at all. The former was divided between admiration of the brilliancy which exercise had given to her complexion, and doubt as to the occasion's justifying her coming so far alone. The latter was thinking only of his breakfast.

Her inquiries after her sister were not very favourably answered. Miss Bennet had slept ill, and though up, was very feverish, and not well enough to leave her room. Elizabeth was glad to be taken to her immediately; and Jane, who had only been withheld by the fear of giving alarm or inconvenience from expressing in her note how much she longed for such a visit, was delighted at her entrance. She was not equal, however, to much conversation, and when Miss Bingley left them together, could attempt little besides expressions of gratitude for the extraordinary kindness she was treated with. Elizabeth silently attended her.

Analysis: The presentation of Elizabeth walking 'alone' to assist her ailing sister at Netherfield is instructive: the main protagonist is presented as being vigorous, vivacious, unpredictable, determined, dismissive of lady-like conventions and highly attractive. Again notice Austen's sentence structure, leaving the most important details until last; Elizabeth is described as having 'weary ankles, dirty stockings, and a face glowing with the warmth of exercise.' The radiant face is crucial in suggesting Elizabeth's sexual allure, her vigour, indicating that she is a girl of vital parts.

Discussion point How does Elizabeth's behaviour here contrast with the other female characters in novel?

Questions

What is the "entail"? What does it mean for the Bennet sisters?

Why do Lydia and Kitty increase their visits to Mrs Phillips, their aunt?

What does Mr Bennet complain about regarding Lydia and Kitty? What does Mrs Bennet think of her two youngest daughters?

What invitation does Jane receive?

Why does Mrs Bennet tell Jane to go by horse?

What happens to Jane on her way to Netherfield? Why does Jane have to stay longer at Netherfield?

What does Elizabeth do when she hears about Jane? What are the Bingley sisters shocked by when she arrives?

Why does Elizabeth end up staying the night at Netherfield?

You can find the answers for the above questions embedded in the chapter summaries on the **Gradesaver website here**.

GCSE style question: how does Austen create both comedy and suspense in this chapter?

Creative response: write Elizabeth's diary for this chapter, recording her feelings about her sisters, Jane's illness, and her visit to Netherfield.

Chapter 8

Extract

When dinner was over, she returned directly to Jane, and Miss Bingley began abusing her as soon as she was out of the room. Her manners were pronounced to be very bad indeed, a mixture of pride and impertinence; she had no conversation, no style, no beauty. Mrs. Hurst thought the same, and added:

"She has nothing, in short, to recommend her, but being an excellent walker. I shall never forget her appearance this morning. She really looked almost wild."

"She did, indeed, Louisa. I could hardly keep my countenance. Very nonsensical to come at all! Why must *she* be scampering about the country, because her sister had a cold? Her hair, so untidy, so blowsy!"

"Yes, and her petticoat; I hope you saw her petticoat, six inches deep in mud, I am absolutely certain; and the gown which had been let down to hide it not doing its office."

"Your picture may be very exact, Louisa," said Bingley; "but this was all lost upon me. I thought Miss Elizabeth Bennet looked remarkably well when she came into the room this morning. Her dirty petticoat quite escaped my notice."

"*You* observed it, Mr. Darcy, I am sure," said Miss Bingley; "and I am inclined to think that you would not wish to see *your* sister make such an exhibition."

"Certainly not."

"To walk three miles, or four miles, or five miles, or whatever it is, above her ankles in dirt, and alone, quite alone! What could she mean by it? It seems to me to show an abominable sort of conceited independence, a most country-town indifference to decorum."

"It shows an affection for her sister that is very pleasing," said Bingley.

Analysis: Mrs Hurst's description of Elizabeth being 'almost wild' reveals that our heroine has entered a society which is constricted and constrained by notions of decorum which stop girls doing vital things such as 'exercise'. Thus Austen subtly paints a portrait an aristocratic society which almost being strangulated by tradition and antiquated custom. This is a society where it is not seemly for a woman to take a walk in bad weather, even for a good cause. Once again, Austen is building up suspense by presenting us with ironic contrasts: the 'style' and 'taste' of Miss Bingley forms a great contrast with the 'pride' and 'impertinence' of Elizabeth. Here we can see how different characters have different uses for the word 'pride'; the Hertfordshire community described Darcy in this way because he was too attached to his aristocratic ways to notice them, while Elizabeth is described as being 'proud' because she is 'common'.

Discussion point: What are the shades of meaning of the abstract noun 'pride' in this novel'?

Questions

How and why does Caroline Bingley criticize Elizabeth?
What do Bingley and Darcy admire about Elizabeth?
How do the Bingley sisters mock the Bennet family?
When Elizabeth joins the conversation, what do Darcy and she argue about? What does Elizabeth reveal during the conversation?
What does Elizabeth feel is ridiculous about Caroline and Darcy's criteria for being an accomplished woman?
A Level/GCSE style question: how does Austen reveal Elizabeth's wit and intelligence in this chapter?
Creative response: write Caroline Bingley's diary entry for this chapter, talking about what she thinks of Jane and Elizabeth.

Chapter 9

Extract

Lydia was a stout, well-grown girl of fifteen, with a fine complexion and good-humoured countenance; a favourite with her mother, whose affection had brought her into public at an early age. She had high animal spirits, and a sort of natural self-consequence, which the attention of the officers, to whom her uncle's good dinners, and her own easy manners recommended her, had increased into assurance. She was very equal, therefore, to address Mr. Bingley on the subject of the ball, and abruptly reminded him of his promise; adding, that it would be the most shameful thing in the world if he did not keep it.

Analysis: The description of Lydia suggests that she is sexually attractive; 'well-grown' intimates that she is fully developed, while the word 'fine complexion' indicates she is very healthy. Furthermore, the noun phrase 'high animal spirits' reveals that she has a 'wild' side, which Elizabeth clearly does not. Her insistence that Bingley should hold a ball shows us that she is rather rude. Here we can see that Austen is showing us that the Netherfield perceptions of Elizabeth are incorrect because now we are introduced to a character who is indeed 'impertinent' and 'wild', and lacking in 'style' and 'taste'. Thus we can see that Austen does not actually think that these concepts are without worth; it's just that the author clearly presents us with people who apply the terms inaccurately.

Discussion point: How and why does the presentation of Lydia contrast with Jane and Elizabeth?

His answer to this sudden attack was delightful to their mother's ear:

Questions

Who does Elizabeth insist visits Netherfield? What is Bingley's response?

Why is Mrs Bennet pleased when she sees Jane regarding the state of her health?

What does everyone at Netherfield realise about Mrs Bennet's intentions?

How does Mrs Bennet treat Darcy?

Why is Elizabeth embarrassed by her mother's behaviour?

GCSE style question: how does Austen create comedy and suspense through her depiction of Mrs Bennet in this chapter?

Creative response: write Mrs Bennet's diary entry for this chapter, outlining her thoughts and feelings about Jane, Elizabeth, Bingley and Darcy. Try and capture the comic tone of the novel.

Chapter 10

Extract

After playing some Italian songs, Miss Bingley varied the charm by a lively Scotch air; and soon afterwards Mr. Darcy, drawing near Elizabeth, said to her:

"Do not you feel a great inclination, Miss Bennet, to seize such an opportunity of dancing a reel?"

She smiled, but made no answer. He repeated the question, with some surprise at her silence.

"Oh!" said she, "I heard you before, but I could not immediately determine what to say in reply. You wanted me, I know, to say 'Yes,' that you might have the pleasure of despising my taste; but I always delight in overthrowing those kind of schemes, and cheating a person of their premeditated contempt. I have, therefore, made up my mind to tell you, that I do not want to dance a reel at all—and now despise me if you dare."

"Indeed I do not dare."

Elizabeth, having rather expected to affront him, was amazed at his gallantry; but there was a mixture of sweetness and archness in her manner which made it difficult for her to affront anybody; and Darcy had never been so bewitched by any woman as he was by her. He really believed, that were it not for the inferiority of her connections, he should be in some danger.

Analysis: Austen has carefully presented Darcy's growing obsession with Elizabeth. Now it is fully fledged in its physical incarnation; clearly the protagonist is intensely attracted to Elizabeth. Once again, notice how the third person voice successfully shifts from showing us how Elizabeth is now becoming aware that she is an object of desire to giving us Darcy's perspective. We are told that he 'had never been so bewitched by any woman' and that believes that 'were it not for the inferiority of her connections, he should be in some danger'. What is fascinating here is the nature of Austen's ironic voice; we are aware that Darcy's desire for Elizabeth is going to conquer his desire to adhere to the conventions of his class, which insist that he marries an aristocratic woman. Thus we see how Austen presents his desire as 'transgressive'; his feelings are in direct contradiction to the wishes of the society he lives in.

Discussion point: How effective is Austen's presentation of Darcy's predicament here?

Questions

How does Caroline flirt with Darcy while he writes a letter to his sister?
What does the group mock Bingley for?
How does Elizabeth defend Bingley?
As the Bingley sisters sing and play the piano, what does Elizabeth notice Darcy is doing?
Why does Elizabeth refuse to dance with Darcy?
What does Caroline notice about Darcy and Elizabeth? How does she mock Darcy in private?
GCSE style question: how does Austen reveal Darcy's growing obsession with Elizabeth in this chapter?
Creative response: write Darcy's diary for this chapter, exploring his changing feelings for Elizabeth.

Chapter 11

Questions

How is Jane feeling after dinner? What pleases Elizabeth when she observes Bingley and Jane?
How does Caroline behave with Darcy? What does she do to try and attract his attention?
What does Caroline eventually do which attracts Darcy's attention?
What does Darcy admit that he has a tendency to do?
What does Elizabeth criticize Darcy for?
You can find the answers for the above questions embedded in the chapter summaries on the **Gradesaver website here**.

GCSE style question: how does Austen reveal the developing relationship between Darcy and Elizabeth in this chapter?

Creative response: write a short story called 'The argument' about an argument between a man/boy and woman/girl in which they argue over how men and women should behave.

Chapter 12

Extract

The master of the house heard with real sorrow that they were to go so soon, and repeatedly tried to persuade Miss Bennet that it would not be safe for her—that she was not enough recovered; but Jane was firm where she felt herself to be right.

To Mr. Darcy it was welcome intelligence—Elizabeth had been at Netherfield long enough. She attracted him more than he liked—and Miss Bingley was uncivil to *her*, and more teasing than usual to himself. He wisely resolved to be particularly careful that no sign of admiration should *now* escape him, nothing that could elevate her with the hope of influencing his felicity; sensible that if such an idea had been suggested, his behaviour during the last day must have material weight in confirming or crushing it. Steady to his purpose, he scarcely spoke ten words to her through the whole of Saturday, and though they were at one time left by themselves for half-an-hour, he adhered most conscientiously to his book, and would not even look at her.

Analysis: Here we can see Austen the acute psychologist and storyteller coming to the fore: Darcy's refusal to look at Elizabeth is because he finds himself too attracted to her. Notice the ironic use of the adverb 'wisely' – here we are entering Darcy's mind, his own interior monologue about how he should deal with his desire towards Elizabeth. Furthermore, we have a real insight into his pride when he decides not to show his admiration for her because he does not want to 'elevate her with the hope of influencing his felicity.' In other words, he does not want her to pay any attention to him because it might inflame him further; it is clear that he is not thinking of her here and the disappointment that she might feel if she is 'led on' and then 'dropped'. In such a way, we can see Austen beginning to sketch out a moral framework for Darcy's development; by the end of the novel, Darcy will have the faculty of empathy, of placing himself in other people's shoes, and thereby losing his 'pride'. For Austen, pride is about being 'inconsiderate', putting one's notions of grandiosity above the feelings of other people.

Discussion point: What do you think of the presentation of Darcy here?

Questions

What do the Bennets plan to do when Jane has recovered?
Why is Mrs Bennet unwilling to send for a carriage?
Whose carriage do the girls ask to borrow?
Who is the only person sorry to see Jane and Elizabeth go?
Why is Darcy glad to see the back of Elizabeth?
Why is Caroline pleased Elizabeth has left?

You can find the answers for the above questions embedded in the chapter summaries on the **Gradesaver website here**.

GCSE style question: how does Austen maintain narrative tension in this chapter?

Creative response: write Elizabeth's diary for this chapter, exploring her mixed feelings about leaving Netherfield.

Chapter 13

Extract

Mr. Collins was punctual to his time, and was received with great politeness by the whole family. Mr. Bennet indeed said little; but the ladies were ready enough to talk, and Mr. Collins seemed neither in need of encouragement, nor inclined to be silent himself. He was a tall, heavy-looking young man of five-and-twenty. His air was grave and stately, and his manners were very formal. He had not been long seated before he complimented Mrs. Bennet on having so fine a family of daughters; said he had heard much of their beauty, but that in this instance fame had fallen short of the truth; and added, that he did not doubt her seeing them all in due time disposed of in marriage. This gallantry was not much to the taste of some of his hearers; but Mrs. Bennet, who quarreled with no compliments, answered most readily.

> Analysis: The introduction of Mr Collins at this point is a masterstroke; leaving us in suspense about the nature of Darcy's feelings for Elizabeth, Austen now shifts the scene to the poorly educated, long-winded Collins. There is a real sense of threat behind Austen's satirical portrait because if one of the daughters doesn't marry Collins, it is possible that they will lose Longbourn to him. Austen generates much comedy in creating a uniquely prolix and comic voice for Collins; the comic portrait looks forward towards the sort of grotesques that Dickens will create a few years later. Like the ghastly Uriah Heap in *David Copperfield* in his unctuous tone and long-winded phrases. Austen's description of him is revealing: he is 'heavy-looking' – in other words, fat and ugly – and his air is 'grave and stately', in other words awkward, gauche and inappropriately 'formal'.

Discussion point: Look carefully at his letter. How does Austen create comedy here?

Questions

What does Mr Bennet announce at breakfast?

Why does Mrs Bennet hate Mr Collins?

What does the letter Mr Collins has written to the family reveal about him?

How old is Mr Collins? What is he like? What is his style of talking?

What does Mr Collins say about the entail? What reason does he give for coming to Longbourn?

What does Mr Collins say he admires at dinner?

You can find the answers for the above questions embedded in the chapter summaries on the **Gradesaver website here**.

A Level/GCSE style question: how and why does Austen present the Bennet family as being under threat?

Creative response: write Elizabeth's diary for this chapter, outlining her reaction to Mr Collins.

Chapter 14

Extract

"You judge very properly," said Mr. Bennet, "and it is happy for you that you possess the talent of flattering with delicacy. May I ask whether these pleasing attentions proceed from the impulse of the moment, or are the result of previous study?"

"They arise chiefly from what is passing at the time, and though I sometimes amuse myself with suggesting and arranging such little elegant compliments as may be adapted to ordinary occasions, I always wish to give them as unstudied an air as possible."

Mr. Bennet's expectations were fully answered. His cousin was as absurd as he had hoped, and he listened to him with the keenest enjoyment, maintaining at the same time the most resolute composure of countenance, and, except in an occasional glance at Elizabeth, requiring no partner in his pleasure.

Analysis: Only Mr Bennet and Elizabeth realise just how ridiculous Mr Collins is. In this sense, the reader feels flattered; we are as clever as the most intelligent people in the novel because we can clearly see that Mr Collins is a grotesque. We gain though an insight into Mr Bennet's psychology here because we can perceive that he does not need anyone else to share his mirth with, although clearly he enjoys the fact that both he and his daughter can smile behind Collins' back.

Discussion point How effectively does Austen present the father-daughter relationship in this novel?

Questions

What does Mr Collins say about Lady Catherine? Who is she and why does he like her so much? What does he say about Lady Catherine's daughter?

What does Mr Bennet think of Mr Collins?

What does Mr Collins never read? What does he read aloud to the family? What is his tone and approach?

How and why does Lydia interrupt Mr Collins's reading? Why is Mr Collins offended? What game does he suggest playing?

You can find the answers for the above questions embedded in the chapter summaries on the **Gradesaver website here**.

GCSE/A Level style question: How does Austen make Mr Collins such a grotesquely funny character?

Creative response: write Mr Bennet's diary for this chapter, offering his thoughts on his daughters, his wife and Mr Collins.

Chapter 15

Extract

Mr. Collins was not a sensible man, and the deficiency of nature had been but little assisted by education or society; the greatest part of his life having been spent under the guidance of an illiterate and miserly father; and though he belonged to one of the universities, he had merely kept the necessary terms, without forming at it any useful acquaintance.

Analysis: Finally, the narrative voice tells us what we all know, that Collins is not 'sensible'. This adjective is interesting because it has several shades of meaning besides the one we have for it today. In particular, it means that Collins is not 'sensitive' of other people's feelings. In some ways, he is 'sensible' – he is clearly well aware about how to look after himself – but he is definitely not empathetic; he has no understanding of other people's feelings.

Discussion point: What does Austen mean by an 'education' do you think?

Extract

His plan did not vary on seeing them. Miss Bennet's lovely face confirmed his views, and established all his strictest notions of what was due to seniority; and for the first evening *she* was his settled choice. The next morning, however, made an alteration; for in a quarter of an hour's tete-a-tete with Mrs. Bennet before breakfast, a conversation beginning with his parsonage-house, and leading naturally to the avowal of his hopes, that a mistress might be found for it at Longbourn, produced from her, amid very complaisant smiles and general encouragement, a caution against the very Jane he had fixed on. "As to her *younger* daughters, she could not take upon her to say—she could not positively answer—but she did not *know* of any prepossession; her *eldest* daughter, she must just mention—she felt it incumbent on her to hint, was likely to be very soon engaged."

Mr. Collins had only to change from Jane to Elizabeth—and it was soon done—done while Mrs. Bennet was stirring the fire. Elizabeth, equally next to Jane in birth and beauty, succeeded her of course.

Analysis: More comedy is generated in Austen's presentation of the fickleness of Collins' feelings, his quickly switching affections from Jane to Elizabeth when he learns that Jane is 'engaged'. Once again, we find Mrs Bennet being the 'puppet-master', the person clearly controlling the situation. In such a way, we see Austen presenting the mother as quite a powerful person at this point in the novel.

Discussion point: How does Austen generate comedy here?

Extract

But the attention of every lady was soon caught by a young man, whom they had never seen before, of most gentlemanlike appearance, walking with another officer on the other side of the way. The officer was the very Mr. Denny concerning whose return from London Lydia came to inquire, and he bowed as they passed. All were struck with the stranger's air, all wondered who he could be; and Kitty and Lydia, determined if possible to find out, led the way across the street, under pretense of wanting something in an opposite shop, and fortunately had just gained the pavement when the two gentlemen, turning back, had reached the same spot. Mr. Denny addressed them directly, and entreated permission to introduce his friend, Mr. Wickham, who had returned with him the day before from town, and he was happy to say had accepted a commission in their corps. This was exactly as it should be; for the young man wanted only regimentals to make him completely charming. His appearance was greatly in his favour; he had all the best part of beauty, a fine countenance, a good figure, and very pleasing address.

Analysis: Austen is a master not only at presenting the intimate feelings of her two protagonists, but also painting a portrait of an entire community. Here we see the world through the eyes of the young ladies of the area, scouring Meryton for officers desperately. Her use of the ironic voice shows though that for all their desperation to see attractive soldiers, there is nothing quite like 'a very smart bonnet' or 'really new muslin'. Having presented us with a threat to the Bennet household in the form of Mr Collins, Austen now introduces us to an even greater one, Mr Wickham. Again notice how Austen uses 'binary opposites' to create a real sense of suspense; Wickham is the opposite to Collins in every way. He has 'the best part of beauty, a fine countenance, a good figure and very pleasing address.' He has none of the appalling pomposity of Collins – but none of his money either.

Discussion point: Why does Austen introduce Wickham at this point?

Questions

What do we learn about Mr Collins's past from the narrator? How does he intend to make amends for the entailment?

Who attracts Mr Collins first? Why does he shift his attentions to Elizabeth?

Who does Mr Collins join on a walk to Meryton? Who do they meet as they walk?

Who is Mr Wickham? What does Elizabeth notice about Mr Darcy and Mr Wickham?

Who does Jane introduce Mr Collins to?

Who does Mrs Phillips, the girls' aunt, intend to invite to dinner the next night?

You can find the answers for the above questions embedded in the chapter summaries on the **Gradesaver website here**.

GCSE style question: how does Austen create mystery and intrigue regarding Mr Wickham?

Creative response: write Mr Collins's diary for this chapter and the previous one, outlining his thoughts about his past, Lady Catherine, the Bennet daughters and the entailment.

Chapter 16

Extract

Mr. Wickham was the happy man towards whom almost every female eye was turned, and Elizabeth was the happy woman by whom he finally seated himself; and the agreeable manner in which he immediately fell into conversation, though it was only on its being a wet night, made her feel that the commonest, dullest, most threadbare topic might be rendered interesting by the skill of the speaker.

Analysis: Austen increases the suspense by indicating Elizabeth may well 'fall for Wickham'. We, the reader, have an uneasy sense that this may not be the best course.

Discussion point: How does Austen create suspense here?

Extract

"I have no right to give *my* opinion," said Wickham, "as to his being agreeable or otherwise. I am not qualified to form one. I have known him too long and too well to be a fair judge. It is impossible for *me* to be impartial. But I believe your opinion of him would in general astonish—and perhaps you would not express it quite so strongly anywhere else. Here you are in your own family."

"Upon my word, I say no more *here* than I might say in any house in the neighbourhood, except Netherfield. He is not at all liked in Hertfordshire. Everybody is disgusted with his pride. You will not find him more favourably spoken of by anyone."

Analysis: Ever the acute psychologist, Austen now gives her chief antagonist the virtue of her own psychological gifts; Wickham uses 'reverse psychology' to lure Elizabeth into accepting his opinions of Mr Darcy. He does this by suggesting that he has 'no right to give his opinion', thereby prompting Elizabeth to ask for it.

Discussion point: Elizabeth appears to speak for Hertfordshire here. Why is this?

Extract

"How strange!" cried Elizabeth. "How abominable! I wonder that the very pride of this Mr. Darcy has not made him just to you! If from no better motive, that he should not have been too proud to be dishonest—for dishonesty I must call it."

"It *is* wonderful," replied Wickham, "for almost all his actions may be traced to pride; and pride had often been his best friend. It has connected him nearer with virtue than with any other feeling. But we are none of us consistent, and in his behaviour to me there were stronger impulses even than pride."

"Can such abominable pride as his have ever done him good?"

"Yes. It has often led him to be liberal and generous, to give his money freely, to display hospitality, to assist his tenants, and relieve the poor. Family pride, and *filial* pride—for he is very proud of what his father was—have done this. Not to appear to disgrace his family, to degenerate from the popular qualities, or lose the influence of the Pemberley House, is a powerful motive. He has also *brotherly* pride, which, with *some* brotherly affection, makes him a very kind and careful guardian of his sister, and you will hear him generally cried up as the most attentive and best of brothers."

Analysis: Once again, we see Austen use 'gossip' to generate suspense; we hear how Darcy mistreated Wickham here but are never really given specific details. The whole theme of pride is amplified here; Darcy's pride is that he did not give Wickham the property that he felt he was owed. Elizabeth now extrapolates from this that his proud refusal to give Wickham the property which was 'rightfully' his was actually 'dishonesty' in that he appeared to renege upon his promise. The emotional temperament of the text rises here; Darcy stands accused of being not only proudly aloof but also proudly dishonest.

Discussion point: How does Austen build suspense here?

Extract

Mr. Wickham's attention was caught; and after observing Mr. Collins for a few moments, he asked Elizabeth in a low voice whether her relation was very intimately acquainted with the family of de Bourgh.

"Lady Catherine de Bourgh," she replied, "has very lately given him a living. I hardly know how Mr. Collins was first introduced to her notice, but he certainly has not known her long."

"You know of course that Lady Catherine de Bourgh and Lady Anne Darcy were sisters; consequently that she is aunt to the present Mr. Darcy."

"No, indeed, I did not. I knew nothing at all of Lady Catherine's connections. I never heard of her existence till the day before yesterday."

"Her daughter, Miss de Bourgh, will have a very large fortune, and it is believed that she and her cousin will unite the two estates."

Analysis: The revelation that Darcy is clearly intended to marry Lady Catherine de Bourgh's daughter adds to the sense that Darcy is deceitful; at Netherfield, he may have been merely pretending to be 'available'.

Discussion point: Why does Austen introduce these revelations about Darcy at this point in the novel?

Questions

What does Elizabeth think of Mr Wickham during dinner at Mrs Phillips?

What does Elizabeth learn about Mr Wickham and Darcy? How, according to Wickham, did Darcy treat Wickham? Why, according to Wickham, does Darcy not like him?

What does Elizabeth feel should happen to Darcy, having heard this story? What is Wickham's response?

What does Wickham hint about his relationship with Darcy's sister, Georgiana?

What does Wickham tell Elizabeth about who Darcy is expected to marry?

You can find the answers for the above questions embedded in the chapter summaries on the **Gradesaver website here**.

GCSE style question: how does Austen present Mr Wickham in this chapter?

Creative response: write Elizabeth's diary for this chapter, outlining her feelings for Wickham and Darcy.

Chapter 17

Extract

"I am by no means of the opinion, I assure you," said he, "that a ball of this kind, given by a young man of character, to respectable people, can have any evil tendency; and I am so far from objecting to dancing myself, that I shall hope to be honoured with the hands of all my fair cousins in the course of the evening; and I take this opportunity of soliciting yours, Miss Elizabeth, for the two first dances especially, a preference which I trust my cousin Jane will attribute to the right cause, and not to any disrespect for her."

Elizabeth felt herself completely taken in. She had fully proposed being engaged by Mr. Wickham for those very dances; and to have Mr. Collins instead! her liveliness had never been worse timed. There was no help for it, however. Mr. Wickham's happiness and her own were perforce delayed a little longer, and Mr. Collins's proposal accepted with as good a grace as she could.

Analysis: Austen presents Elizabeth as being almost smitten with Wickham; she wishes to have "two dances" with him – always an indication of true attraction. Once again, the ironic voice shies away from describing her feelings directly but rather indicating that they are strong because she can not "help" asking Collins whether he intends to accept the invitation.

Discussion point: How and why does Austen shy away from describing Elizabeth's feelings directly?

Questions

What is Jane's response when Elizabeth tells her about Darcy and Wickham?

What do Mr Bingley and his sisters announce that causes great excitement?

Why does Mr Collins want to go to the ball? Why is Elizabeth disappointed by this news? Who does Elizabeth want to dance with at the ball?

What does Elizabeth realise about Mr Collins's intentions towards her? How does she respond to Collins?

You can find the answers for the above questions embedded in the chapter summaries on the **Gradesaver website here**.

GCSE style question: how does Austen reveal the plight of women in her society in this chapter?

Creative response: write a part one of a story called 'The Ball' or 'The Party' etc, in which some girls/boys learn that there is going to be a big party, and wonder who they will dance/go with etc.

Chapter 18

Extract

Till Elizabeth entered the drawing-room at Netherfield, and looked in vain for Mr. Wickham among the cluster of red coats there assembled, a doubt of his being present had never occurred to her. The certainty of meeting him had not been checked by any of those recollections that might not unreasonably have alarmed her. She had dressed with more than usual care, and prepared in the highest spirits for the conquest of all that remained unsubdued of his heart, trusting that it was not more than might be won in the course of the evening. But in an instant arose the dreadful suspicion of his being purposely omitted for Mr. Darcy's pleasure in the Bingleys' invitation to the officers; and though this was not exactly the case, the absolute fact of his absence was pronounced by his friend Denny, to whom Lydia eagerly applied, and who told them that Wickham had been obliged to go to town on business the day before, and was not yet returned; adding, with a significant smile, "I do not imagine his business would have called him away just now, if he had not wanted to avoid a certain gentleman here."

Analysis: The absence of Wickham is the first in a series of narrative twists regarding this chief antagonist. Wickham is shrouded in mystery in much the same way that Frank Churchill will come to be in *Emma*. Moreover, Elizabeth decides to jump to conclusions about him in much the same way that Emma does with Frank Churchill.

Discussion point: Why is Elizabeth's suspicion 'dreadful'?

Extract

The effect was immediate. A deeper shade of *hauteur* overspread his features, but he said not a word, and Elizabeth, though blaming herself for her own weakness, could not go on. At length Darcy spoke, and in a constrained manner said, "Mr. Wickham is blessed with such happy manners as may ensure his *making* friends—whether he may be equally capable of *retaining* them, is less certain."

"He has been so unlucky as to lose *your* friendship," replied Elizabeth with emphasis, "and in a manner which he is likely to suffer from all his life."

Darcy made no answer, and seemed desirous of changing the subject. At that moment, Sir William Lucas appeared close to them, meaning to pass through the set to the other side of the room; but on perceiving Mr. Darcy, he stopped with a bow of superior courtesy to compliment him on his dancing and his partner.

Analysis: Austen generates more mystery and tension by presenting us with Darcy appearing 'constrained' when talking about Wickham.

Discussion point: What are the reader's feelings towards Darcy at this point?

Extract

"So, Miss Eliza, I hear you are quite delighted with George Wickham! Your sister has been talking to me about him, and asking me a thousand questions; and I find that the young man quite forgot to tell you, among his other communication, that he was the son of old Wickham, the late Mr. Darcy's steward. Let me recommend you, however, as a friend, not to give implicit confidence to all his assertions; for as to Mr. Darcy's using him ill, it is perfectly false; for, on the contrary, he has always been remarkably kind to him, though George Wickham has treated Mr. Darcy in a most infamous manner. I do not know the particulars, but I know very well that Mr. Darcy is not in the least to blame, that he cannot bear to hear George Wickham mentioned, and that though my brother thought that he could not well avoid including him in his invitation to the officers, he was excessively glad to find that he had taken himself out of the way.

Analysis: Miss Bingley's intervention is unexpected; the reader cannot be sure if she is well-meaning or not. She is evidently anxious to clear Darcy's name, but we have to suspect her motives as she is a suitor for Darcy's hand in marriage. The intervention gives her some depth, taking her beyond the 'bitchy' stereotype we have hitherto seen.

Discussion point: What do you think of the way Austen presents Miss Bingley here?

Extract

"What is Mr. Darcy to me, pray, that I should be afraid of him? I am sure we owe him no such particular civility as to be obliged to say nothing *he* may not like to hear."

"For heaven's sake, madam, speak lower. What advantage can it be for you to offend Mr. Darcy? You will never recommend yourself to his friend by so doing!"

Nothing that she could say, however, had any influence. Her mother would talk of her views in the same intelligible tone. Elizabeth blushed and blushed again with shame and vexation. She could not help frequently glancing her eye at Mr. Darcy, though every glance convinced her of what she dreaded; for though he was not always looking at her mother, she was convinced that his attention was invariably fixed by her. The expression of his face changed gradually from indignant contempt to a composed and steady gravity.

Analysis: Here we see Elizabeth and Darcy's perceptions to almost imperceptibly converge; it is clear that they both feel ashamed of the behaviour of Mrs Bennet, who in crowing about the forthcoming marriage of Jane to Bingley appears to be counting her chickens. The pair are beginning to share the same outlook; to implicitly build a morality around manners. Good manners for Elizabeth and Darcy mean not 'showing off' or being presumptuous.

Discussion point: Would Mrs Bennet's behaviour be so shameful now? What would the modern equivalent be?

Questions

Whose absence disappoints Elizabeth when she arrives at the ball? Why does she assume this person has stayed away?

Who does she dance two dances with? How does Elizabeth find these dances?

Who shocks her by asking her to dance?

How does Elizabeth poke fun at Darcy? What does she accuse him of?

What is the mood when Darcy and Elizabeth part?

What does Caroline warn Jane Elizabeth must be careful of? What does Caroline say about Wickham and Darcy?

When Jane tells Elizabeth about what Caroline thinks of Wickham, how does Elizabeth react? What does Jane tell Elizabeth about Bingley's views of Wickham? What is Elizabeth's reaction to this news?

What does Mr Collins learn about Mr Darcy's relationship with Lady Catherine? What is his reaction? What does Elizabeth warn Mr Collins about?

How do Jane and Bingley get on during the evening?

What is Mrs Bennet thrilled about?

How and why does Mrs Bennet embarrass Elizabeth?

How does Mary embarrass the Bennet family? How does Elizabeth manage to stop this embarrassment?

How does Mr Collins further embarrass the Bennet family?

Who does Mrs Bennet invite to dinner at the end of the evening? What does she feel sure will happen soon?

You can find the answers for the above questions embedded in the chapter summaries on the **Gradesaver website here**.

A Level/GCSE style question: how does Austen make the ball such an exciting and comedic scene in the novel?

Creative response: write Elizabeth's diary for this scene, making sure you discuss her feelings for Wickham, Darcy, her family and Mr Collins.

Chapter 19

Extract

The next day opened a new scene at Longbourn. Mr. Collins made his declaration in form. Having resolved to do it without loss of time, as his leave of absence extended only to the following Saturday, and having no feelings of diffidence to make it distressing to himself even at the moment, he set about it in a very orderly manner, with all the observances, which he supposed a regular part of the business. On finding Mrs. Bennet, Elizabeth, and one of the younger girls together, soon after breakfast, he addressed the mother in these words:

"May I hope, madam, for your interest with your fair daughter Elizabeth, when I solicit for the honour of a private audience with her in the course of this morning?"

Before Elizabeth had time for anything but a blush of surprise, Mrs. Bennet answered instantly, "Oh dear!—yes—certainly. I am sure Lizzy will be very happy—I am sure she can have no objection. Come, Kitty, I want you up stairs." And, gathering her work together, she was hastening away, when Elizabeth called out:

"Dear madam, do not go. I beg you will not go. Mr. Collins must excuse me. He can have nothing to say to me that anybody need not hear. I am going away myself."

Analysis: Mrs Bennet remains a powerful figure here, engineering in a somewhat sinister if very obvious fashion the possible engagement between Elizabeth and Mr Collins.

Discussion point: Mrs Bennet is both a comic and powerful figure at this point. How sinister is she?

Extract

"I do assure you, sir, that I have no pretensions whatever to that kind of elegance which consists in tormenting a respectable man. I would rather be paid the compliment of being believed sincere. I thank you again and again for the honour you have done me in your proposals, but to accept them is absolutely impossible. My feelings in every respect forbid it. Can I speak plainer? Do not consider me now as an elegant female, intending to plague you, but as a rational creature, speaking the truth from her heart."

"You are uniformly charming!" cried he, with an air of awkward gallantry; "and I am persuaded that when sanctioned by the express authority of both your excellent parents, my proposals will not fail of being acceptable."

To such perseverance in wilful self-deception Elizabeth would make no reply, and immediately and in silence withdrew; determined, if he persisted in considering her repeated refusals as flattering encouragement, to apply to her father, whose negative might be uttered in such a manner as to be decisive, and whose behaviour at least could not be mistaken for the affectation and coquetry of an elegant female.

Analysis: There is much comedy in this first proposal scene in the novel. Collins' refusal to believe that Elizabeth has rejected him reveals him to be both absurd and deluded. However, he does echo some fundamental prejudices that men have about women, namely that they mean the opposite to what they say particularly when talking about their sexuality. The 'coquetry of an elegant female' is such that it was not the fashionable thing to accept a first proposal of marriage. This scene is very important because it reveals a penniless woman rejecting the advances of a relatively wealthy man. Fifty years before Elizabeth would not have had the right to reject Collins because marriage was perceived primarily to be a business agreement; a way of securing a safe financial future. The pressure is very much upon her at this point because the family may lose Longbourn if she does not marry Collins.

Discussion point: How and why does Austen create tension and comedy in this first marriage scene?

Questions

Who does Mr Collins propose to and why? What reason does he give for wanting to marry her?

What is Elizabeth's response? How does Mr Collins react? What reasons does he give for her rejection?

Why does Elizabeth leave the room in the end?

You can find the answers for the above questions embedded in the chapter summaries on the **Gradesaver website here**.

GCSE style question: how does Austen make the proposal such a comic and tense moment in the novel?

Creative response: write Elizabeth's diary for this chapter, outlining her reaction to Mr Collins's proposal.

Chapter 20

Extract

Mrs. Bennet rang the bell, and Miss Elizabeth was summoned to the library.

"Come here, child," cried her father as she appeared. "I have sent for you on an affair of importance. I understand that Mr. Collins has made you an offer of marriage. Is it true?" Elizabeth replied that it was. "Very well—and this offer of marriage you have refused?"

"I have, sir."

"Very well. We now come to the point. Your mother insists upon your accepting it. Is it not so, Mrs. Bennet?"

"Yes, or I will never see her again."

"An unhappy alternative is before you, Elizabeth. From this day you must be a stranger to one of your parents. Your mother will never see you again if you do *not* marry Mr. Collins, and I will never see you again if you *do*."

Elizabeth could not but smile at such a conclusion of such a beginning, but Mrs. Bennet, who had persuaded herself that her husband regarded the affair as she wished, was excessively disappointed.

Analysis: From this moment on, Mrs Bennet becomes a deflated figure; it is clear that she does not have the backing of her husband in her plans and that she is not the more powerful person in the relationship when it comes to the crunch. Her threats are revealed finally to be what they are; toothless. With his famous over-ruling of his wife, Mr Bennet establishes his true authority. As with so many of Austen's great quotations, it is the last words in the sentence which create its emphatic effect. When he says, *"I will never see you again if you do"* we see how the sentence operates on the basis of antithesis; almost word for word it contradicts everything he describes his wife as believing in the first part of the sentence. It is a perfectly balanced sentence. It carries a heavy emotional punch too because we have been genuinely worried that Elizabeth will be trapped in a loveless, horrific marriage with the monstrous Mr Collins.

Discussion point: What do you think of the way that Austen presents the Bennets in this extract?

Questions

How does Mrs Bennet react when she learns that Elizabeth has rejected

Mr Collins? What does she tell Mr Bennet to do?

What does Mr Bennet say to Elizabeth when he speaks to her about Mr Collins's proposal?

Why does Mrs Bennet argue with Elizabeth?

Who comes to visit the house during this turmoil?

What does Mr Collins accept by the end of the chapter?

You can find the answers for the above questions embedded in the chapter summaries on the **Gradesaver website here**.

GCSE style question: look carefully at the scene when Mr Bennet talks to Elizabeth about Mr Collins's proposal. How does Austen make this both a funny and moving scene?

Creative response: write Mr Bennet's diary for this chapter, outlining his thoughts about his wife and his daughters.

Chapter 21

Extract

"Mr. Darcy is impatient to see his sister; and, to confess the truth, *we* are scarcely less eager to meet her again. I really do not think Georgiana Darcy has her equal for beauty, elegance, and accomplishments; and the affection she inspires in Louisa and myself is heightened into something still more interesting, from the hope we dare entertain of her being hereafter our sister. I do not know whether I ever before mentioned to you my feelings on this subject; but I will not leave the country without confiding them, and I trust you will not esteem them unreasonable. My brother admires her greatly already; he will have frequent opportunity now of seeing her on the most intimate footing; her relations all wish the connection as much as his own; and a sister's partiality is not misleading me, I think, when I call Charles most capable of engaging any woman's heart. With all these circumstances to favour an attachment, and nothing to prevent it, am I wrong, my dearest Jane, in indulging the hope of an event which will secure the happiness of so many?"

"What do you think of *this* sentence, my dear Lizzy?" said Jane as she finished it. "Is it not clear enough? Does it not expressly declare that Caroline neither expects nor wishes me to be her sister; that she is perfectly convinced of her brother's indifference; and that if she suspects the nature of my feelings for him, she means (most kindly!) to put me on my guard? Can there be any other opinion on the subject?"

Analysis: Now that Elizabeth and her father have decidedly rejected Mr Collins, another less tangible rejection begins to seep into the text; Mr Bingley's rejection of Jane. This will occupy much of the rest of the novel; Bingley's absence will cast a pall over many of the ensuing chapters, bringing misery to the normally even-tempered and equitable Jane. Added to this complication is the shadow of Miss

Darcy, who appears to be a much more suitable match for Darcy being rich and from a higher class than him.

Discussion point: Why does Austen introduce the notion of Bingley's rejection of Jane so soon after Elizabeth has rejected Collins?

Questions

How does Mr Collins now treat Elizabeth?

What do you notice about Wickham and Elizabeth's relationship during this chapter?

What does Caroline Bingley's letter tell Jane? Who is Bingley likely to marry? How does Jane react?

How does Elizabeth try and comfort Jane? What does Elizabeth believe Bingley will do?

You can find the answers for the above questions embedded in the chapter summaries on the **Gradesaver website here**.

A Level/GCSE style question: how does Austen present Jane in this chapter?

Creative response: write Jane's diary for this chapter, outlining her feelings and thoughts about Bingley.

Chapter 22

Extract

In as short a time as Mr. Collins's long speeches would allow, everything was settled between them to the satisfaction of both; and as they entered the house he earnestly entreated her to name the day that was to make him the happiest of men; and though such a solicitation must be waived for the present, the lady felt no inclination to trifle with his happiness. The stupidity with which he was favoured by nature must guard his courtship from any charm that could make a woman wish for its continuance; and Miss Lucas, who accepted him solely from the pure and disinterested desire of an establishment, cared not how soon that establishment were gained.

Sir William and Lady Lucas were speedily applied to for their consent; and it was bestowed with a most joyful alacrity. Mr. Collins's present circumstances made it a most eligible match for their daughter, to whom they could give little fortune; and his prospects of future wealth were exceedingly fair. Lady Lucas began directly to calculate, with more interest than the matter had ever excited before, how many years longer Mr. Bennet was likely to live; and Sir William gave it as his decided opinion, that whenever Mr. Collins should be in possession of the Longbourn estate, it would be highly expedient that both he and his wife should make their appearance at St. James's. The whole family, in short, were properly overjoyed on the occasion. The younger girls formed hopes of *coming out* a year or two sooner than they might otherwise have done; and the boys were relieved from their apprehension of Charlotte's dying an old maid. Charlotte herself was tolerably composed. She had gained her point, and had time to consider of it. Her reflections were in general satisfactory. Mr. Collins, to be sure, was neither sensible nor agreeable; his society was irksome, and his attachment to her must be imaginary. But still he would be her husband. Without thinking highly either of men or matrimony, marriage had always been her object; it was the only provision for well-educated young women of small fortune, and however uncertain of giving happiness, must be their pleasantest preservative from want. This preservative she had now obtained; and at the age of twenty-seven, without having ever been handsome, she felt all the good luck of it. The least agreeable circumstance in the business was the surprise it must occasion to Elizabeth Bennet, whose friendship she valued beyond that of any other person.

Analysis: Austen offers us another narrative twist here with the 'kind' Charlotte Lucas becoming engaged to Mr Collins. Austen generates more comedy by making a striking contrast between Collins' long-winded way of talking and the speed with which he 'escapes' out of Longbourn House once he relies his best bet is to marry Charlotte. The oxymoronic noun phrase 'admirable slyness' is, of course, ironic because it is clear to us that Collins is very far from admirable but he is most definitely 'sly' – for all his stupidity, he is selfishly cunning. Austen's use of this oxymoron draws attention to a more sinister aspect in Collins' character; he is ruthless and without consideration for other people. In this sense, we are pleased he marries Charlotte because she is a close friend of Lizzie's and is unlikely to 'turf' the Bennet family out of house and home when Mr Bennet dies. There is a poignancy about the engagement; Charlotte at twenty seven has resigned herself to being an 'old maid' – most women married in their late teens and early twenties. Moreover, somewhat shockingly Collins at twenty five is younger than her. This suggestions that Charlotte knows she has to marry Collins because she will receive no other offers.

Discussion point: To what extent is Charlotte's engagement to Mr Collins believable? What does it tell us about Charlotte and Mr Collins?

Extract

The possibility of Mr. Collins's fancying himself in love with her friend had once occurred to Elizabeth within the last day or two; but that Charlotte could encourage him seemed almost as far from possibility as she could encourage him herself, and her astonishment was consequently so great as to overcome at first the bounds of decorum, and she could not help crying out:

"Engaged to Mr. Collins! My dear Charlotte—impossible!"

The steady countenance which Miss Lucas had commanded in telling her story, gave way to a momentary confusion here on receiving so direct a reproach; though, as it was no more than she expected, she soon regained her composure, and calmly replied:

"Why should you be surprised, my dear Eliza? Do you think it incredible that Mr. Collins should be able to procure any woman's good opinion, because he was not so happy as to succeed with you?"

But Elizabeth had now recollected herself, and making a strong effort for it, was able to assure with tolerable firmness that the prospect of their relationship was highly grateful to her, and that she wished her all imaginable happiness.

Analysis: Here we see Charlotte gently castigating Elizabeth's 'prejudice' against Mr Collins. The dialogue is dramatic and realistic, as well as reflective; looking back over a major event. It also reveals to us a strong friendship under strain.

Discussion point: How effective is Austen's presentation of the friendship between Charlotte and Elizabeth here?

Questions

Who does Charlotte talk to for the rest of the day? Why?

Who does Mr Collins propose to and why?

Why is Mr Collins quite rude in the way he leaves Longbourn?

Why is Elizabeth shocked at news of this engagement? Why is she disappointed with Charlotte?

You can find the answers for the above questions embedded in the chapter summaries on the **Gradesaver website here**.

GCSE style question: how does Austen make Mr Collins develop into a sinister character?

Creative response: write Charlotte Lucas's diary for this chapter, outlining her reasons for wanting to marry Mr Collins.

Chapter 23

Questions

What does Sir William Lucas announce when he arrives at Longbourn? What is the family's reaction?

After recovering from her disbelief, why does Mrs Bennet become angry with Elizabeth?

How does Elizabeth and Charlotte's relationship change now?

Why are Elizabeth and Jane concerned by the lack of news from Bingley?

Who returns to Longbourn? How do the family treat him?

You can find the answers for the above questions embedded in the chapter summaries on the **Gradesaver website here**.

GCSE style question: how does Austen portray the relationship between Elizabeth and her mother in the preceding chapters? Think back across all your reading.

Chapter 24

Extract

Miss Bingley's letter arrived, and put an end to doubt. The very first sentence conveyed the assurance of their being all settled in London for the winter, and concluded with her brother's regret at not having had time to pay his respects to his friends in Hertfordshire before he left the country.

Hope was over, entirely over; and when Jane could attend to the rest of the letter, she found little, except the professed affection of the writer, that could give her any comfort. Miss Darcy's praise occupied the chief of it. Her many attractions were again dwelt on, and Caroline boasted joyfully of their increasing intimacy, and ventured to predict the accomplishment of the wishes which had been unfolded in her former letter.

Analysis: The atmosphere of high comedy which had permeated the beginning of the book has now disappeared; it is clear that Bingley has rejected Jane as a possible wife. Miss Bingley appears to be a formidable adversary; she boasts "joyfully" of the "increasing intimacy" between her and Miss Darcy. In other words, the Bingleys are being inducted into the ways of the aristocracy and that it appears likely that Miss Bingley will marry Darcy, and Miss Darcy will marry Bingley. The writing is very powerful here because we feel the full impact of Jane's disappointment; she is relatively poor and without a hope now of marrying the man she loves.

Discussion point: How and why does Austen a real sense of disappointment at this point in the novel?

Questions

What does Caroline Bingley's letter to Jane tell her? What does Caroline boast about in her letter?

What does Jane talk about to Elizabeth in private? What does Elizabeth say Caroline and Darcy have done to Bingley? What is Jane's response?

Why does Mrs Bennet upset Jane?

Who visits and cheers up the Bennet family?

Because of Wickham's stories, what do most of Hertfordshire believe about Mr Darcy?

You can find the answers for the above questions embedded in the

chapter summaries on the **Gradesaver website here.**

A Level style question: how does Austen manage to create narrative intrigue in this chapter?

Chapter 25

Extract

When alone with Elizabeth afterwards, she spoke more on the subject. "It seems likely to have been a desirable match for Jane," said she. "I am sorry it went off. But these things happen so often! A young man, such as you describe Mr. Bingley, so easily falls in love with a pretty girl for a few weeks, and when accident separates them, so easily forgets her, that these sort of inconsistencies are very frequent."

"An excellent consolation in its way," said Elizabeth, "but it will not do for *us*. We do not suffer by *accident*. It does not often happen that the interference of friends will persuade a young man of independent fortune to think no more of a girl whom he was violently in love with only a few days before."

"But that expression of 'violently in love' is so hackneyed, so doubtful, so indefinite, that it gives me very little idea. It is as often applied to feelings which arise from a half-hour's acquaintance, as to a real, strong attachment. Pray, how *violent was* Mr. Bingley's love?"

"I never saw a more promising inclination; he was growing quite inattentive to other people, and wholly engrossed by her.

> Analysis: As if to add insult to injury, Mrs Bennet rubs in the disappointment with her 'many grievances' and complaints. She is the opposite of a supportive parent, clearly blaming both daughters for failing to marry. We can gather a sense of Elizabeth's shock in the way she says she "never saw a more promising inclination". Since the reader now trusts Elizabeth as a fine psychologist, we realise that Bingley is making a mistake in rejecting Jane. If Elizabeth is to be trusted, he was really in love with her.

> Discussion point: What do you think of the way Austen presents the aftermath of the rejection?

Extract

The Gardiners stayed a week at Longbourn; and what with the Phillipses, the Lucases, and the officers, there was not a day without its engagement. Mrs. Bennet had so carefully provided for the entertainment of her brother and sister, that they did not once sit down to a family dinner. When the engagement was for home, some of the officers always made part of it—of which officers Mr. Wickham was sure to be one; and on these occasions, Mrs. Gardiner, rendered suspicious by Elizabeth's warm commendation, narrowly observed them both. Without supposing them, from what she saw, to be very seriously in love, their preference of each other was plain enough to make her a little uneasy; and she resolved to speak to Elizabeth on the subject before she left Hertfordshire, and represent to her the imprudence of encouraging such an attachment.

To Mrs. Gardiner, Wickham had one means of affording pleasure, unconnected with his general powers. About ten or a dozen years ago, before her marriage, she had spent a considerable time in that very part of Derbyshire to which he belonged. They had, therefore, many acquaintances in common; and though Wickham had been little there since the death of Darcy's father, it was yet in his power to give her fresher intelligence of her former friends than she had been in the way of procuring.

Mrs. Gardiner had seen Pemberley, and known the late Mr. Darcy by character perfectly well. Here consequently was an inexhaustible subject of discourse. In comparing her recollection of Pemberley with the minute description which Wickham could give, and in bestowing her tribute of praise on the character of its late possessor, she was delighting both him and herself. On being made acquainted with the present Mr. Darcy's treatment of him, she tried to remember some of that gentleman's reputed disposition when quite a lad which might agree with it, and was confident at last that she recollected having heard Mr. Fitzwilliam Darcy formerly spoken of as a very proud, ill-natured boy.

Analysis: Austen builds more suspense here by presenting us with Mrs Gardiner who knows of the situation between Darcy and Wickham. Mrs Gardiner's belief that Wickham was the wronged party lends weight to the impression that Darcy is "very proud". However, Mrs Gardiner is keen to steer Elizabeth away from Wickham, who she suspects of being an unsuitable match. Elizabeth takes her advice and loses her interest in him. Since this is a comedy, Austen turns the days following Bingley's rejection of Jane into a social whirl, dispelling the mood of gloom that has settled over the novel.

Discussion point: Why does Austen present us with Mrs Gardiner at this point?

Questions

How does Mr Collins leave Longbourn?

Who visits after he leaves? What are they like as people?

What does Elizabeth tell Mrs Gardiner about Jane and Bingley? How does Mrs Gardiner offer to help?

What does Mrs Gardiner observe is happening between Elizabeth and Wickham?

Why does Mrs Gardiner enjoy talking to Wickham?

You can find the answers for the above questions embedded in the

chapter summaries on the **Gradesaver website here.**

A Level/GCSE style question: how does Mrs Gardiner add more interest to the story?

Creative response: write Mrs Gardiner's diary for this chapter, talking about her feelings towards the Bennet family and Wickham.

Chapter 26

Extract

This letter gave Elizabeth some pain; but her spirits returned as she considered that Jane would no longer be duped, by the sister at least. All expectation from the brother was now absolutely over. She would not even wish for a renewal of his attentions. His character sunk on every review of it; and as a punishment for him, as well as a possible advantage to Jane, she seriously hoped he might really soon marry Mr. Darcy's sister, as by Wickham's account, she would make him abundantly regret what he had thrown away.

Analysis: Austen manages to make Jane a rounded character because we do see her suffer real disappointment; she has travelled to London in an attempt to see the Bingleys and ascertain what the status of her relationship with them is. She is bitterly hurt when they refuse to see her, despite the fact that they are in town. Here finally Jane acknowledges the truth about Miss Bingley and her engagement to Bingley; she realises she has been rejected.

Discussion point: How effective is Austen's characterization of Jane Bennet?

Questions

What does Mrs Gardiner warn Elizabeth of? What does Elizabeth promise to do?

Who gets married next?

What does Jane's letter inform Elizabeth about the way Caroline Bingley has treated Jane in London? What happened between Caroline and Jane?

What does Elizabeth's letter inform Mrs Gardiner about regarding her feelings for Wickham?

You can find the answers for the above questions embedded in the chapter summaries on the **Gradesaver website here.**

A Level/GCSE style question: how does Austen make letters so entertaining for the reader in the novel so far?

Creative response: write Elizabeth's diary for this chapter, exploring her changing feelings for Wickham.

Chapter 27

Extract

Her fellow-travellers the next day were not of a kind to make her think him less agreeable. Sir William Lucas, and his daughter Maria, a good-humoured girl, but as empty-headed as himself, had nothing to say that could be worth hearing, and were listened to with about as much delight as the rattle of the chaise. Elizabeth loved absurdities, but she had known Sir William's too long. He could tell her nothing new of the wonders of his presentation and knighthood; and his civilities were worn out, like his information.

It was a journey of only twenty-four miles, and they began it so early as to be in Gracechurch Street by noon. As they drove to Mr. Gardiner's door, Jane was at a drawing-room window watching their arrival; when they entered the passage she was there to welcome them, and Elizabeth, looking earnestly in her face, was pleased to see it healthful and lovely as ever. On the stairs were a troop of little boys and girls, whose eagerness for their cousin's appearance would not allow them to wait in the drawing-room, and whose shyness, as they had not seen her for a twelvemonth, prevented their coming lower. All was joy and kindness. The day passed most pleasantly away; the morning in bustle and shopping, and the evening at one of the theatres.

Analysis: The novel is, for all that it is predominantly set in Hertfordshire, virtually a 'travelogue' as well, with the characters traversing the country. Here we see Elizabeth visiting Mrs Gardiner in the City of London on her way to Kent to see her friend Charlotte and Mr Collins. She sees her sister again and realises that Jane is quite resilient, being in good spirits despite the rejection.

Discussion point: Why does Austen shift the scene to London at this point?

Questions

On what terms do Elizabeth and Wickham part?

Who does Elizabeth set off to Hunsford with? Who do they visit on their way in London?

What does Elizabeth learn about Jane's state of mind from Mrs Gardiner?

What does Mrs Gardiner believe Wickham is doing with Miss King? How does Elizabeth react to this news?

What do the Gardiners invite Elizabeth to do? What is her response?

You can find the answers for the above questions embedded in the chapter summaries on the **Gradesaver website here.**

GCSE style question: what effect do the different settings in this novel have upon the reader?

Creative response: write Elizabeth's diary for this chapter, outlining her thoughts on her travels, Jane, Mrs Gardiner and Wickham.

Chapter 28

Extract

The evening was spent chiefly in talking over Hertfordshire news, and telling again what had already been written; and when it closed, Elizabeth, in the solitude of her chamber, had to meditate upon Charlotte's degree of contentment, to understand her address in guiding, and composure in bearing with, her husband, and to acknowledge that it was all done very well. She had also to anticipate how her visit would pass, the quiet tenor of their usual employments, the vexatious interruptions of Mr. Collins, and the gaieties of their intercourse with Rosings. A lively imagination soon settled it all.

Analysis: Unlike Hertfordshire, this area of Kent is dominated by the aristocratic home of Lady Catherine de Bourgh; Mr Collins is an "establishment" member of the church who feels that he owes his status and livelihood to Lady Catherine. There is almost something blasphemous in his worship of her; she has the quality of a living, breathing God to him.

Discussion point: How does Austen build suspense here?

Extract

About the middle of the next day, as she was in her room getting ready for a walk, a sudden noise below seemed to speak the whole house in confusion; and, after listening a moment, she heard somebody running up stairs in a violent hurry, and calling loudly after her. She opened the door and met Maria in the landing place, who, breathless with agitation, cried out—

"Oh, my dear Eliza! pray make haste and come into the dining-room, for there is such a sight to be seen! I will not tell you what it is. Make haste, and come down this moment."

Elizabeth asked questions in vain; Maria would tell her nothing more, and down they ran into the dining-room, which fronted the lane, in quest of this wonder; It was two ladies stopping in a low phaeton at the garden gate.

"And is this all?" cried Elizabeth. "I expected at least that the pigs were got into the garden, and here is nothing but Lady Catherine and her daughter."

Analysis: Elizabeth's exclamation shows her level-headed attitude towards the aristocracy; she is resolutely unimpressed by their airs and graces.

Discussion point: How does Austen generate comedy here?

Questions

How does Mr Collins greet Elizabeth, Sir William and Maria?

How does Charlotte treat her new husband? What does she enjoy doing? How well does Elizabeth think Charlotte is doing?

Who do they find waiting outside their house in a carriage? What does Elizabeth think of this person in the carriage?

Why does Elizabeth think Miss de Bourgh's ill health will affect Darcy if he marries her?

You can find the answers for the above questions embedded in the chapter summaries on the **Gradesaver website here.**

GCSE style question: how does Austen present the upper classes in this novel?

Creative response: write Austen's diary for this chapter, talking about her reaction to Miss de Bourgh's health.

Chapter 29

Extract

When, after examining the mother, in whose countenance and deportment she soon found some resemblance of Mr. Darcy, she turned her eyes on the daughter, she could almost have joined in Maria's astonishment at her being so thin and so small. There was neither in figure nor face any likeness between the ladies. Miss de Bourgh was pale and sickly; her features, though not plain, were insignificant; and she spoke very little, except in a low voice, to Mrs. Jenkinson, in whose appearance there was nothing remarkable, and who was entirely engaged in listening to what she said, and placing a screen in the proper direction before her eyes.

Analysis: The presentation of Miss de Bourgh is shocking; this daughter of the all-powerful Lady Catherine is "pale and sickly", speaking in a "low voice". Critics have speculated that embedded in this description is an implicit criticism of aristocratic inbreeding; the snobbery and social exclusivity of the de Bourghs has led to a genetic 'weakening' of the line. Once again we see Austen inviting contrasts with Elizabeth, who memorably after her walk to Netherfield in the first part of the novel, appeared so vigorous and full of life. By marrying Elizabeth, Darcy will re-inject the line with fresh blood and avoid the dangers of inbreeding.

Discussion point: What do you think of the presentation of Miss de Bourgh and Lady Catherine?

Extract

'Lady Catherine,' said she, 'you have given me a treasure.' Are any of your younger sisters out, Miss Bennet?"

"Yes, ma'am, all."

"All! What, all five out at once? Very odd! And you only the second. The younger ones out before the elder ones are married! Your younger sisters must be very young?"

"Yes, my youngest is not sixteen. Perhaps *she* is full young to be much in company. But really, ma'am, I think it would be very hard upon younger sisters, that they should not have their share of society and amusement, because the elder may not have the means or inclination to marry early. The last-born has as good a right to the pleasures of youth as the first. And to be kept back on *such* a motive! I think it would not be very likely to promote sisterly affection or delicacy of mind."

"Upon my word," said her ladyship, "you give your opinion very decidedly for so young a person. Pray, what is your age?"

"With three younger sisters grown up," replied Elizabeth, smiling, "your ladyship can hardly expect me to own it."

Lady Catherine seemed quite astonished at not receiving a direct answer; and Elizabeth suspected herself to be the first creature who had ever dared to trifle with so much dignified impertinence.

"You cannot be more than twenty, I am sure, therefore you need not conceal your age."

"I am not one-and-twenty."

Analysis: Austen creates real tension when dramatising the conversations between Elizabeth and Lady Catherine; Elizabeth avoids answering her directly and appears not to be bullied by her. Lady Catherine is astonished at Elizabeth's 'dignified impertinence'. When the aristocratic woman says, "You give your opinion very decidedly for so young a person" we sense that the novel has shifted from being a social comedy to being a description of a subtle class and generational battle. Elizabeth represents the 'new' rising mercantile class – that Austen herself was part of – which has gained status through being intelligent, industrious and adroit, while de Bourgh represents the older, aristocratic generation which is stifled by its obsession with convention and pride.

Discussion point: How does Austen generate suspense in her presentation of the conversation between Elizabeth and Lady Catherine?

Questions

What does Mr Collins say about Rosings?

What is Lady Catherine like in person? What is her daughter like?

What questions does Lady Catherine ask Elizabeth? How and why does she come across as rude?

What does Catherine think of Elizabeth's attitude?

You can find the answers for the above questions embedded in the chapter summaries on the **Gradesaver website here.**

A Level/GCSE style question: how does Austen present the de Bourgh family in this chapter?

Creative response: write Elizabeth's diary, discussing her thoughts and feelings about Rosings, Lady Catherine and her daughter.

Chapter 30

Extract

In this quiet way, the first fortnight of her visit soon passed away. Easter was approaching, and the week preceding it was to bring an addition to the family at Rosings, which in so small a circle must be important. Elizabeth had heard soon after her arrival that Mr. Darcy was expected there in the course of a few weeks, and though there were not many of her acquaintances whom she did not prefer, his coming would furnish one comparatively new to look at in their Rosings parties, and she might be amused in seeing how hopeless Miss Bingley's designs on him were, by his behaviour to his cousin, for whom he was evidently destined by Lady Catherine, who talked of his coming with the greatest satisfaction, spoke of him in terms of the highest admiration, and seemed almost angry to find that he had already been frequently seen by Miss Lucas and herself.

His arrival was soon known at the Parsonage; for Mr. Collins was walking the whole morning within view of the lodges opening into Hunsford Lane, in order to have the earliest assurance of it, and after making his bow as the carriage turned into the Park, hurried home with the great intelligence. On the following morning he hastened to Rosings to pay his respects. There were two nephews of Lady Catherine to require them, for Mr. Darcy had brought with him a Colonel Fitzwilliam, the younger son of his uncle Lord ——, and, to the great surprise of all the party, when Mr. Collins returned, the gentlemen accompanied him.

Analysis: Austen deftly now starts drawing the narrative together with the return of Darcy, clearing the way for the confrontation between Elizabeth and him.

Discussion point: Why do you think that Austen introduces Darcy back into the narrative at this point?

Questions

How does Elizabeth pass her time at Hunsford? What are the dinners at Rosings like?

Who is planning to visit Rosings? Why is Elizabeth looking forward to this visitor coming?

What is Darcy's response when Elizabeth asks him about Jane?

You can find the answers for the above questions embedded in the chapter summaries on the **Gradesaver website here.**

A Level/GCSE style question: how does Austen reveal Darcy and Elizabeth's growing closeness in this chapter?

Creative response: write Darcy's diary for this chapter, outlining his thoughts and feelings about Rosings, Lady Catherine and her daughter, and Elizabeth.

Chapter 31

Extract

"You mean to frighten me, Mr. Darcy, by coming in all this state to hear me? I will not be alarmed though your sister *does* play so well. There is a stubbornness about me that never can bear to be frightened at the will of others. My courage always rises at every attempt to intimidate me."

"I shall not say you are mistaken," he replied, "because you could not really believe me to entertain any design of alarming you; and I have had the pleasure of your acquaintance long enough to know that you find great enjoyment in occasionally professing opinions which in fact are not your own."

Elizabeth laughed heartily at this picture of herself, and said to Colonel Fitzwilliam, "Your cousin will give you a very pretty notion of me, and teach you not to believe a word I say. I am particularly unlucky in meeting with a person so able to expose my real character, in a part of the world where I had hoped to pass myself off with some degree of credit. Indeed, Mr. Darcy, it is very ungenerous in you to mention all that you knew to my disadvantage in Hertfordshire—and, give me leave to say, very impolitic too—for it is provoking me to retaliate, and such things may come out as will shock your relations to hear."

"I am not afraid of you," said he, smilingly.

> Analysis: This bristling encounter is now charged with the weight of what has gone before in the narrative; Austen introduces Colonel Fitzwilliam as a somewhat bemused onlooker who does not understand the reasons behind the animosity between Darcy and Elizabeth.

Discussion point: How does Austen create humour and emotional intensity in the above encounter?

Extract

"My fingers," said Elizabeth, "do not move over this instrument in the masterly manner which I see so many women's do. They have not the same force or rapidity, and do not produce the same expression. But then I have always supposed it to be my own fault—because I will not take the trouble of practising. It is not that I do not believe *my* fingers as capable as any other woman's of superior execution."

Darcy smiled and said, "You are perfectly right. You have employed your time much better. No one admitted to the privilege of hearing you can think anything wanting. We neither of us perform to strangers."

Here they were interrupted by Lady Catherine, who called out to know what they were talking of. Elizabeth immediately began playing again. Lady Catherine approached, and, after listening for a few minutes, said to Darcy:

"Miss Bennet would not play at all amiss if she practised more, and could have the advantage of a London master. She has a very good notion of fingering, though her taste is not equal to Anne's. Anne would have been a delightful performer, had her health allowed her to learn."

Analysis: Here we see that Elizabeth is not a 'finished' lady in the way that Miss de Bourgh is because she has not, by her own admission, practised enough. She is an expressive but not so fluent player. Again, we can see that Elizabeth and the author place more emphasis upon the way she plays rather than her technique. Elizabeth is an intelligent player rather than a robotic one.

Discussion point: Why and how does Austen create tension over piano playing?

Questions

Why does Lady Catherine stop inviting Elizabeth and the Collinses to dinner for a week?

When Elizabeth does visit Rosings, how does Lady Catherine behave towards her? What does Darcy think of his aunt's behaviour?

How do Elizabeth and Darcy behave towards each other at the piano?

What aspect of Elizabeth does Lady Catherine criticize?

What observations does Elizabeth make of Darcy's treatment of Miss de Bourgh?

You can find the answers for the above questions embedded in the chapter summaries on the **Gradesaver website here.**

A Level/GCSE style question: How does Austen represent Darcy as a sympathetic and sensitive person in this chapter?

Creative response: write a story called 'She/he had it in for me' which contains a similar situation to the one described in this chapter where there is a person like Lady Catherine who has a grudge against the protagonist.

Chapter 32

Extract

Mr. Darcy drew his chair a little towards her, and said, "*You* cannot have a right to such very strong local attachment. *You* cannot have been always at Longbourn."

Elizabeth looked surprised. The gentleman experienced some change of feeling; he drew back his chair, took a newspaper from the table, and glancing over it, said, in a colder voice:

"Are you pleased with Kent?"

A short dialogue on the subject of the country ensued, on either side calm and concise—and soon put an end to by the entrance of Charlotte and her sister, just returned from her walk. The tete-a-tete surprised them. Mr. Darcy related the mistake which had occasioned his intruding on Miss Bennet, and after sitting a few minutes longer without saying much to anybody, went away.

Analysis: Here Austen presents Darcy's ambivalent feelings towards Elizabeth by showing them to us in the way he moves his chair. First of all, he moves towards her, indicating his attraction for her, then he draws away and reads the newspaper. Thus we can see him battling with his feelings; his heart is telling him to be with Elizabeth, but his head is making him pull away.

Discussion point: What do you think of the presentation of Darcy at this point?

"

Questions

When Darcy visits the next morning, how does he behave around Elizabeth and why?

What advice does Darcy give Elizabeth? What is Elizabeth's response?

What does Charlotte Lucas think Darcy feels towards Elizabeth? What is Elizabeth's response?

What does Elizabeth think Colonel Fitzwilliam feels towards her?

Why do you think Darcy visits so often? What does Charlotte keep suggesting the reason is? What is Elizabeth's response?

GCSE style question: how does Austen maintain the narrative suspense in this chapter?

Creative response: write Elizabeth's diary for this chapter, exploring her thoughts and feelings about Darcy.

Chapter 33

Extract

More than once did Elizabeth, in her ramble within the park, unexpectedly meet Mr. Darcy. She felt all the perverseness of the mischance that should bring him where no one else was brought, and, to prevent its ever happening again, took care to inform him at first that it was a favourite haunt of hers.

Analysis: Here again, we gain a growing sense of Darcy's obsession for Elizabeth and her lack of awareness that he is attracted to her.

Discussion point: What do we feel towards Elizabeth and Darcy at this point?

Extract

"Did Mr. Darcy give you reasons for this interference?"

"I understood that there were some very strong objections against the lady."

"And what arts did he use to separate them?"

"He did not talk to me of his own arts," said Fitzwilliam, smiling. "He only told me what I have now told you."

Elizabeth made no answer, and walked on, her heart swelling with indignation. After watching her a little, Fitzwilliam asked her why she was so thoughtful.

"I am thinking of what you have been telling me," said she. "Your cousin's conduct does not suit my feelings. Why was he to be the judge?"

"You are rather disposed to call his interference officious?"

"I do not see what right Mr. Darcy had to decide on the propriety of his friend's inclination, or why, upon his own judgement alone, he was to determine and direct in what manner his friend was to be happy. But," she continued, recollecting herself, "as we know none of the particulars, it is not fair to condemn him. It is not to be supposed that there was much affection in the case."

"That is not an unnatural surmise," said Fitzwilliam, "but it is a lessening of the honour of my cousin's triumph very sadly."

This was spoken jestingly; but it appeared to her so just a picture of Mr. Darcy, that she would not trust herself with an answer, and therefore, abruptly changing the conversation talked on indifferent matters until they reached the Parsonage. There, shut into her own room, as soon as their visitor left them, she could think without interruption of all that she had heard.

Analysis: The tension mounts in Kent as Elizabeth finds that she is still bumping into Darcy despite the fact that she has warned about where she walks, believing that he will then avoid her. Now Fitzwilliam tells her the story behind Bingley rejecting Jane. There is a heavy element of dramatic irony here because we have lived through the emotional trauma of the rejection; what Fitzwilliam summarises in a few words has been 'lived out' in many previous chapters.

Discussion point: Why does Austen present Darcy in such an unfavourable light at this point?

Questions

Why do you think Elizabeth frequently meets Darcy on his walks? What happens when they meet?

What hints about marriage does Darcy drop in this chapter? How does Elizabeth misunderstand him?

What does Colonel Fitzwilliam tell Elizabeth about the reasons why he has not married? What does he tell her about Darcy advising Bingley over marriage? What is Elizabeth's response?

You can find the answers for the above questions embedded in the chapter summaries on the **Gradesaver website here.**

GCSE style question: how does Austen explore the theme of marriage in this chapter?

Creative response: write Elizabeth's diary for this chapter, in which she reflects upon Darcy and Colonel Fitzwilliam.

Chapter 34

Extract

In spite of her deeply-rooted dislike, she could not be insensible to the compliment of such a man's affection, and though her intentions did not vary for an instant, she was at first sorry for the pain he was to receive; till, roused to resentment by his subsequent language, she lost all compassion in anger. She tried, however, to compose herself to answer him with patience, when he should have done. He concluded with representing to her the strength of that attachment which, in spite of all his endeavours, he had found impossible to conquer; and with expressing his hope that it would now be rewarded by her acceptance of his hand. As he said this, she could easily see that he had no doubt of a favourable answer. He *spoke* of apprehension and anxiety, but his countenance expressed real security. Such a circumstance could only exasperate farther, and, when he ceased, the colour rose into her cheeks, and she said:

"In such cases as this, it is, I believe, the established mode to express a sense of obligation for the sentiments avowed, however unequally they may be returned. It is natural that obligation should be felt, and if I could *feel* gratitude, I would now thank you. But I cannot—I have never desired your good opinion, and you have certainly bestowed it most unwillingly.

Analysis: Here we come to the most dramatic part of the book, Darcy's first proposal to Elizabeth. At this point both characters embody the title of the novel; Darcy is full of pride and Elizabeth is prejudiced against him and his class. Her rejection of him is perhaps less shocking for a modern audience, but it would have been for Austen's readers; such a favourable match would not have been rejected by most women. Darcy is presented as a deeply conflicted man who is aware of Elizabeth's 'inferiority' and the 'degradation' that his desire for entails. Her forthright reply, 'I never desired your good opinion, and you have certainly bestowed it most unwillingly...' works on many levels. On one level, she does not like his presumptuousness; he presumes that he can have her because he has a good opinion of her, but on another level, we see how she does not understand fully the nature of his desire or her own.

Discussion point: How does Austen create drama and tension here?

Extract

"You take an eager interest in that gentleman's concerns," said Darcy, in a less tranquil tone, and with a heightened colour.

"Who that knows what his misfortunes have been, can help feeling an interest in him?"

"His misfortunes!" repeated Darcy contemptuously; "yes, his misfortunes have been great indeed."

"And of your infliction," cried Elizabeth with energy. "You have reduced him to his present state of poverty—comparative poverty. You have withheld the advantages which you must know to have been designed for him. You have deprived the best years of his life of that independence which was no less his due than his desert. You have done all this! and yet you can treat the mention of his misfortune with contempt and ridicule."

"And this," cried Darcy, as he walked with quick steps across the room, "is your opinion of me! This is the estimation in which you hold me! I thank you for explaining it so fully. My faults, according to this calculation, are heavy indeed! But perhaps," added he, stopping in his walk, and turning towards her, "these offenses might have been overlooked, had not your pride been hurt by my honest confession of the scruples that had long prevented my forming any serious design. These bitter accusations might have been suppressed, had I, with greater policy, concealed my struggles, and flattered you into the belief of my being impelled by unqualified, unalloyed inclination; by reason, by reflection, by everything. But disguise of every sort is my abhorrence. Nor am I ashamed of the feelings I related. They were natural and just. Could you expect me to rejoice in the inferiority of your connections?—to congratulate myself on the hope of relations, whose condition in life is so decidedly beneath my own?"

Elizabeth felt herself growing more angry every moment; yet she tried to the utmost to speak with composure when she said:

"You are mistaken, Mr. Darcy, if you suppose that the mode of your declaration affected me in any other way, than as it spared me the concern which I might have felt in refusing you, had you behaved in a more gentlemanlike manner."

She saw him start at this, but he said nothing, and she continued:

"You could not have made the offer of your hand in any possible way that would have tempted me to accept it."

Again his astonishment was obvious; and he looked at her with an expression of mingled incredulity and mortification. She went on:

"From the very beginning—from the first moment, I may almost say—of my acquaintance with you, your manners, impressing me with the fullest belief of your arrogance, your conceit, and your selfish disdain of the feelings of others, were such as to form the groundwork of disapprobation on which succeeding events have built so immovable a dislike; and I had not known you a month before I felt that you were the last man in the world whom I could ever be prevailed on to marry."

"You have said quite enough, madam. I perfectly comprehend your feelings, and have now only to be ashamed of what my own have been. Forgive me for having taken up so much of your time, and accept my best wishes for your health and happiness."

And with these words he hastily left the room, and Elizabeth heard him the next moment open the front door and quit the house.

The tumult of her mind, was now painfully great. She knew not how to support herself, and from actual weakness sat down and cried for half-an-hour.

Analysis: Her rejection of him is decisive and a climatic point in the book; all Elizabeth's prejudices towards Darcy are now in the open, and his pride is manifest for her to see.

Discussion point: How effective is Austen's presentation of

Questions

Who surprises Elizabeth by calling? What is his manner like?

What does Darcy tell Elizabeth about his feelings? How and why does he offend Elizabeth?

Why does Elizabeth reject Darcy's proposal? Give her three reasons for doing so.

What is Darcy's response?

What does Elizabeth do when he is gone? Why does she decide she must not regret her rejection of him?

You can find the answers for the above questions embedded in the chapter summaries on the **Gradesaver website here.**

GCSE/A Level question: how does Austen make Darcy's first proposal such a dramatic, emotional and comedic moment?

Creative response: write Elizabeth or Darcy's diary for this section, exploring their thoughts and feelings about the marriage proposal. Or write a story called 'The Proposal' where everything goes wrong; it does not have to be a marriage proposal.

Chapter 35

Extract:

Darcy's letter:

"The part which I acted is now to be explained. His sisters' uneasiness had been equally excited with my own; our coincidence of feeling was soon discovered, and, alike sensible that no time was to be lost in detaching their brother, we shortly resolved on joining him directly in London. We accordingly went—and there I readily engaged in the office of pointing out to my friend the certain evils of such a choice. I described, and enforced them earnestly. But, however this remonstrance might have staggered or delayed his determination, I do not suppose that it would ultimately have prevented the marriage, had it not been seconded by the assurance that I hesitated not in giving, of your sister's indifference. He had before believed her to return his affection with sincere, if not with equal regard. But Bingley has great natural modesty, with a stronger dependence on my judgement than on his own. To convince him, therefore, that he had deceived himself, was no very difficult point. To persuade him against returning into Hertfordshire, when that conviction had been given, was scarcely the work of a moment. I cannot blame myself for having done thus much. There is but one part of my conduct in the whole affair on which I do not reflect with satisfaction; it is that I condescended to adopt the measures of art so far as to conceal from him your sister's being in town. I knew it myself, as it was known to Miss Bingley; but her brother is even yet ignorant of it. That they might have met without ill consequence is perhaps probable; but his regard did not appear to me enough extinguished for him to see her without some danger. Perhaps this concealment, this disguise was beneath me; it is done, however, and it was done for the best. On this subject I have nothing more to say, no other apology to offer. If I have wounded your sister's feelings, it was unknowingly done and though the motives which governed me may to you very naturally appear insufficient, I have not yet learnt to condemn them.

Analysis: Letters play a very important part in the novel, but this is by far the most important letter, this is the letter which actually 'heals' the rift between Elizabeth and Darcy because it shows two things; Darcy's newly 'humble' state, deprived of pride, and it exposes Elizabeth's prejudice.

Discussion point: In what way do we see in the language of the letter that Darcy has lost his pride?

Extract:

Darcy's letter :

"This, madam, is a faithful narrative of every event in which we have been concerned together; and if you do not absolutely reject it as false, you will, I hope, acquit me henceforth of cruelty towards Mr. Wickham. I know not in what manner, under what form of falsehood he had imposed on you; but his success is not perhaps to be wondered at. Ignorant as you previously were of everything concerning either, detection could not be in your power, and suspicion certainly not in your inclination.

"You may possibly wonder why all this was not told you last night; but I was not then master enough of myself to know what could or ought to be revealed. For the truth of everything here related, I can appeal more particularly to the testimony of Colonel Fitzwilliam, who, from our near relationship and constant intimacy, and, still more, as one of the executors of my father's will, has been unavoidably acquainted with every particular of these transactions. If your abhorrence of *me* should make *my* assertions valueless, you cannot be prevented by the same cause from confiding in my cousin; and that there may be the possibility of consulting him, I shall endeavour to find some opportunity of putting this letter in your hands in the course of the morning. I will only add, God bless you.

"FITZWILLIAM DARCY"

Analysis: Here the wickedness of Wickham comes to light and we realise why Darcy was reluctant to reveal this information because it involved the dishonour of his sister. Some critics have said that the novel is structurally flawed because this letter effectively ends the conflict between Elizabeth and Darcy and yet the novel still is in mid-flow. As a result, Austen has to invent all sorts of sub-plots to keep Elizabeth and Darcy apart until the end, plots which do not enrich the central themes of pride and prejudice.

Discussion point: Why and how does Austen now reveal Wickham to be a villain? Does this letter come too early in the novel?

Questions

Who does Elizabeth meet on her walk? What does he give her?

What reasons does Darcy give for persuading Bingley not to marry Jane? How did Darcy's father try to help Wickham?

What did Darcy give Wickham after Darcy's father died? What did Wickham do as a result of this gift? What did Wickham ask Darcy for and what was Darcy's response?

What did Wickham do with Georgiana Darcy? How old was she? Why does Darcy think Wickham wanted Georgiana?

You can find the answers for the above questions embedded in the chapter summaries on the **Gradesaver website here.**

A Level/GCSE style question: how does Austen create narrative tension with Darcy's letter?

Creative response: write a story called 'The Letter/email' which contains a major revelation.

Chapter 36

Extract:

She grew absolutely ashamed of herself. Of neither Darcy nor Wickham could she think without feeling she had been blind, partial, prejudiced, absurd.

"How despicably I have acted!" she cried; "I, who have prided myself on my discernment! I, who have valued myself on my abilities! who have often disdained the generous candour of my sister, and gratified my vanity in useless or blameable mistrust! How humiliating is this discovery! Yet, how just a humiliation! Had I been in love, I could not have been more wretchedly blind! But vanity, not love, has been my folly. Pleased with the preference of one, and offended by the neglect of the other, on the very beginning of our acquaintance, I have courted prepossession and ignorance, and driven reason away, where either were concerned. Till this moment I never knew myself."

From herself to Jane—from Jane to Bingley, her thoughts were in a line which soon brought to her recollection that Mr. Darcy's explanation *there* had appeared very insufficient, and she read it again. Widely different was the effect of a second perusal. How could she deny that credit to his assertions in one instance, which she had been obliged to give in the other? He declared himself to be totally unsuspicious of her sister's attachment; and she could not help remembering what Charlotte's opinion had always been. Neither could she deny the justice of his description of Jane. She felt that Jane's feelings, though fervent, were little displayed, and that there was a constant complacency in her air and manner not often united with great sensibility.

Analysis: Elizabeth now begins to lose her prejudice and feels ashamed of her past conduct and beliefs. She now begins to see Darcy in a more favourable light.

Discussion point: Why does Austen present Elizabeth like this do you think?

Questions

What is Elizabeth's response to the letter? What points in the letter does she initially not want to accept or believe?

After thinking about the letter for a while, what does she come to realise about the contents of the letter? Why does she begin to doubt Wickham?

What does she begin to feel towards Darcy? What does she realise about herself? What does she accept about the letter regarding Jane, and her mother/sisters?

Who has said goodbye when she returns to the parsonage?

You can find the answers for the above questions embedded in the chapter summaries on the **Gradesaver website here.**

A Level/GCSE style question: how does Austen explore the theme of prejudice in this chapter?

Creative response: write Elizabeth's diary for this chapter, outlining her changing responses to the letter.

Chapter 37

Questions

What can't Elizabeth help thinking as she has dinner with Lady Catherine? What does Lady Catherine attempt to persuade Elizabeth and Mary to do?

What does Elizabeth feel bad about regarding Darcy? What does she begin to realise about Lydia and Kitty? Why does she think her family's behavior might have led to Jane not marrying Bingley?

You can find the answers for the above questions embedded in the chapter summaries on the **Gradesaver website here.**

A Level/GCSE style question: how does Austen explore the thoughts and feelings of Elizabeth in this chapter?

Creative response: write a story/poem called 'My embarrassing family' in which the narrator describes his/her embarrassing family.

Chapter 38

Questions

Where do Elizabeth and Maria visit before going back to Longbourn? Who returns home with them?

Why does Elizabeth not tell Jane about Darcy and his letter

straightaway?

You can find the answers for the above questions embedded in the chapter summaries on the **Gradesaver website here.**

GCSE style question: how does Austen create sympathy for Charlotte in this chapter?

Creative response: write Elizabeth's diary, outlining her response to leaving the parsonage and seeing Jane.

Chapter 39

Extract:

But of this answer Lydia heard not a word. She seldom listened to anybody for more than half a minute, and never attended to Mary at all.

In the afternoon Lydia was urgent with the rest of the girls to walk to Meryton, and to see how everybody went on; but Elizabeth steadily opposed the scheme. It should not be said that the Miss Bennets could not be at home half a day before they were in pursuit of the officers. There was another reason too for her opposition. She dreaded seeing Mr. Wickham again, and was resolved to avoid it as long as possible. The comfort to *her* of the regiment's approaching removal was indeed beyond expression. In a fortnight they were to go—and once gone, she hoped there could be nothing more to plague her on his account.

She had not been many hours at home before she found that the Brighton scheme, of which Lydia had given them a hint at the inn, was under frequent discussion between her parents. Elizabeth saw directly that her father had not the smallest intention of yielding; but his answers were at the same time so vague and equivocal, that her mother, though often disheartened, had never yet despaired of succeeding at last.

Analysis: The threat of Wickham seems to be removed, yet there are hints that all is not because of Lydia's wish to go to Brighton.

Discussion point: Why does Austen present the army as a threat at this point in the novel?

Questions

Why is Elizabeth happy to hear that the regiment will soon be leaving Meryton? Why are Lydia and Kitty upset?

Where is Lydia hoping Mr Bennet will allow them to visit that summer and why?

Who is now available because Miss King has left the area?

What stories does Lydia tell her sisters?

Why does Elizabeth want to stay at home and not go for a walk with her sisters to Meryton?

You can find the answers for the above questions embedded in the chapter summaries on the **Gradesaver website here.**

GCSE style question: how does Austen make Lydia such a lively, irritating and comic figure in this chapter and elsewhere in the novel?

Creative response: write Elizabeth's diary for this section, exploring her feelings towards her sisters and Darcy.

Chapter 40

Extract:

She was now, on being settled at home, at leisure to observe the real state of her sister's spirits. Jane was not happy. She still cherished a very tender affection for Bingley. Having never even fancied herself in love before, her regard had all the warmth of first attachment, and, from her age and disposition, greater steadiness than most first attachments often boast; and so fervently did she value his remembrance, and prefer him to every other man, that all her good sense, and all her attention to the feelings of her friends, were requisite to check the indulgence of those regrets which must have been injurious to her own health and their tranquillity.

Analysis: Here we see how conflicted Elizabeth is by her previous prejudice, not even daring to tell Jane the truth about Bingley's affection for her. It is a chastening experience for Elizabeth.

Discussion point: What do you think of the way Austen presents Elizabeth here?

Questions

What does Elizabeth tell Jane about the next morning? What does she leave out and why?

What really shocks Jane? What do the sister discuss about what they should do regarding Wickham? What do they finally decide?

What does Elizabeth realise about Jane's state of mind and her feelings?

You can find the answers for the above questions embedded in the chapter summaries on the **Gradesaver website here.**

A Level style question: how does Austen present the relationship between Jane and Elizabeth in this chapter?

Creative response: write Jane's diary for this chapter, outlining her response to what Elizabeth tells her about Darcy and Wickham, as well as her feelings towards Bingley.

Chapter 41

Extract:

"You, who so well know my feeling towards Mr. Darcy, will readily comprehend how sincerely I must rejoice that he is wise enough to assume even the *appearance* of what is right. His pride, in that direction, may be of service, if not to himself, to many others, for it must only deter him from such foul misconduct as I have suffered by. I only fear that the sort of cautiousness to which you, I imagine, have been alluding, is merely adopted on his visits to his aunt, of whose good opinion and judgement he stands much in awe. His fear of her has always operated, I know, when they were together; and a good deal is to be imputed to his wish of forwarding the match with Miss de Bourgh, which I am certain he has very much at heart."

Elizabeth could not repress a smile at this, but she answered only by a slight inclination of the head. She saw that he wanted to engage her on the old subject of his grievances, and she was in no humour to indulge him. The rest of the evening passed with the*appearance*, on his side, of usual cheerfulness, but with no further attempt to distinguish Elizabeth; and they parted at last with mutual civility, and possibly a mutual desire of never meeting again.

When the party broke up, Lydia returned with Mrs. Forster to Meryton, from whence they were to set out early the next morning.

> **Analysis:** Here we see that the spell of Wickham has been broken and we realise that he is merely a 'cad'; his 'alarm' and 'heightened complexion' reveal his guilt.

> **Discussion point:** What are our feelings towards Wickham at this point?

The separation between her and her family was rather noisy than pathetic. Kitty was the only one who shed tears; but she did weep from vexation and envy. Mrs. Bennet was diffuse in her good wishes for the felicity of her daughter, and impressive in her injunctions that she should not miss the opportunity of enjoying herself as much as possible—advice which there was every reason to believe would be well attended to; and in the clamorous happiness of Lydia herself in bidding farewell, the more gentle adieus of her sisters were uttered without being heard.

Questions

Why are Kitty, Lydia and Mrs Bennet disappointed? What invitation does Lydia receive?

Why does Elizabeth beg her father to stop Lydia from going? Why does he ignore her advice?

Who does Elizabeth see frequently? What does Elizabeth hint she knows to Wickham? How does Wickham respond?

You can find the answers for the above questions embedded in the chapter summaries on the **Gradesaver website here.**

A Level style essay: how does Austen present Wickham as a slippery and deceitful character in the novel?

Creative response: write Elizabeth's diary for this chapter, outlining her thoughts about Lydia, her father and Wickham.

Chapter 42

Extract:

Elizabeth said no more—but her mind could not acquiesce. The possibility of meeting Mr. Darcy, while viewing the place, instantly occurred. It would be dreadful! She blushed at the very idea, and thought it would be better to speak openly to her aunt than to run such a risk. But against this there were objections; and she finally resolved that it could be the last resource, if her private inquiries to the absence of the family were unfavourably answered.

Accordingly, when she retired at night, she asked the chambermaid whether Pemberley were not a very fine place? what was the name of its proprietor? and, with no little alarm, whether the family were down for the summer? A most welcome negative followed the last question—and her alarms now being removed, she was at leisure to feel a great deal of curiosity to see the house herself; and when the subject was revived the next morning, and she was again applied to, could readily answer, and with a proper air of indifference, that she had not really any dislike to the scheme. To Pemberley, therefore, they were to go.

Analysis: Austen now tries to create suspense by making the reader speculate about what might happen when Darcy and Elizabeth meet at Pemberley. Notice Austen's use of irony here. When the narrator says, 'It would be dreadful!' we realise that we are inside Elizabeth's head. We the reader of course think that the meeting will be extremely exciting.

Discussion point: What do you think of the way the author presents Elizabeth at this point?

Questions

What do we learn about the history of the relationship between Mr and Mrs Bennet? What is Mr Bennet's sole enjoyment now?

How does Elizabeth think her parents' marriage has affected the children? Why does Elizabeth feel her father is at fault?

What makes life at Longbourn difficult?

Why is Elizabeth glad to get away? Where are they going and why?

Where do the travelling party pass nearby?

You can find the answers for the above questions embedded in the chapter summaries on the **Gradesaver website here.**

A Level style question: how does Austen present Mr and Mrs Bennet's marriage in the novel so far?

Creative response: write Kitty's diary, outlining her thoughts about her parents and sisters.

Chapter 43

Extract:

Elizabeth, as they drove along, watched for the first appearance of Pemberley Woods with some perturbation; and when at length they turned in at the lodge, her spirits were in a high flutter.

The park was very large, and contained great variety of ground. They entered it in one of its lowest points, and drove for some time through a beautiful wood stretching over a wide extent.

Elizabeth's mind was too full for conversation, but she saw and admired every remarkable spot and point of view. They gradually ascended for half-a-mile, and then found themselves at the top of a considerable eminence, where the wood ceased, and the eye was instantly caught by Pemberley House, situated on the opposite side of a valley, into which the road with some abruptness wound. It was a large, handsome stone building, standing well on rising ground, and backed by a ridge of high woody hills; and in front, a stream of some natural importance was swelled into greater, but without any artificial appearance. Its banks were neither formal nor falsely adorned. Elizabeth was delighted. She had never seen a place for which nature had done more, or where natural beauty had been so little counteracted by an awkward taste. They were all of them warm in their admiration; and at that moment she felt that to be mistress of Pemberley might be something!

Analysis: Here we see Elizabeth's sense of the grandeur of the property which she might be 'mistress of'. It is interesting to note that Pemberley is pre-dominantly 'natural' in its appearance; the stream 'swells' into a greater one 'without any artificial appearance'. In other words, there is a sense that this is not the false grandeur of Rosings, Lady Catherine's home, but is naturally grand. In other words, unlike Darcy at the beginning of the novel, Pemberley is without 'airs', without 'pride'. This appears to be the reason why Elizabeth is drawn to it; not because it is obviously the home of an extremely wealthy aristocrat.

Discussion point: What do you think of the presentation of Pemberley?

Extract:

The introduction, however, was immediately made; and as she named their relationship to herself, she stole a sly look at him, to see how he bore it, and was not without the expectation of his decamping as fast as he could from such disgraceful companions. That he was *surprised* by the connection was evident; he sustained it, however, with fortitude, and so far from going away, turned back with them, and entered into conversation with Mr. Gardiner. Elizabeth could not but be pleased, could not but triumph. It was consoling that he should know she had some relations for whom there was no need to blush. She listened most attentively to all that passed between them, and gloried in every expression, every sentence of her uncle, which marked his intelligence, his taste, or his good manners.

The conversation soon turned upon fishing; and she heard Mr. Darcy invite him, with the greatest civility, to fish there as often as he chose while he continued in the neighbourhood, offering at the same time to supply him with fishing tackle, and pointing out those parts of the stream where there was usually most sport. Mrs. Gardiner, who was walking arm-in-arm with Elizabeth, gave her a look expressive of wonder. Elizabeth said nothing, but it gratified her exceedingly; the compliment must be all for herself. Her astonishment, however, was extreme, and continually was she repeating, "Why is he so altered? From what can it proceed? It cannot be for *me*—it cannot be for *my* sake that his manners are thus softened. My reproofs at Hunsford could not work such a change as this. It is impossible that he should still love me."

Analysis: Here we see a different Darcy; Elizabeth appears to have cured his insufferable pride. Austen writes of Elizabeth: "she could hardly suppress a smile at his being now seeking the acquaintance of some of those very people against whom his pride had revolted in his offer to herself." We have an overwhelming sense that the couple have 'grown up'. It is perhaps this sort of scene that the 'romantic', possibly female readers of the novel yearn for; Elizabeth has 'moulded' Darcy into a different being. He is clearly still besotted by her.

Discussion point: To what extent is the new Darcy believable? Is this meeting just a romantic fantasy?

Extract:

They now walked on in silence, each of them deep in thought. Elizabeth was not comfortable; that was impossible; but she was flattered and pleased. His wish of introducing his sister to her was a compliment of the highest kind. They soon outstripped the others, and when they had reached the carriage, Mr. and Mrs. Gardiner were half a quarter of a mile behind.

He then asked her to walk into the house—but she declared herself not tired, and they stood together on the lawn. At such a time much might have been said, and silence was very awkward. She wanted to talk, but there seemed to be an embargo on every subject. At last she recollected that she had been travelling, and they talked of Matlock and Dove Dale with great perseverance. Yet time and her aunt moved slowly—and her patience and her ideas were nearly worn out before the tete-a-tete was over. On Mr. and Mrs. Gardiner's coming up they were all pressed to go into the house and take some refreshment; but this was declined, and they parted on each side with utmost politeness. Mr. Darcy handed the ladies into the carriage; and when it drove off, Elizabeth saw him walking slowly towards the house.

> Analysis: Darcy has become a romantic hero by now, 'walking slowly towards the house'.

> Discussion point: Look back at the scenes in Pemberley. How has the novel shifted in tone and approach?

Questions

What does Elizabeth like about Pemberley? What is she beginning to regret?

How does the housekeeper, Mrs Reynolds, present Darcy? What surprises Elizabeth about this description?

When Darcy appears, how does he behave with Elizabeth and the Gardiners? What is Elizabeth worried he might think about her?

Why is Elizabeth surprised by the way Darcy talks to the Gardiners? What does Darcy invite Mr Gardiner to do?

When Elizabeth and Darcy talk, who does he say he will introduce her to?

Why are the Gardiners surprised by Darcy?

You can find the answers for the above questions embedded in the chapter summaries on the **Gradesaver website here.**

A Level style question: how and why does Austen present Pemberley in the way she does?

Creative response: write Elizabeth's diary for this chapter, outlining her response to Pemberley.

Chapter 44

Extract:

In seeing Bingley, her thoughts naturally flew to her sister; and, oh! how ardently did she long to know whether any of his were directed in a like manner. Sometimes she could fancy that he talked less than on former occasions, and once or twice pleased herself with the notion that, as he looked at her, he was trying to trace a resemblance. But, though this might be imaginary, she could not be deceived as to his behaviour to Miss Darcy, who had been set up as a rival to Jane. No look appeared on either side that spoke particular regard. Nothing occurred between them that could justify the hopes of his sister.

Analysis: The novel now continues its 'upward' path towards achieving the happiness of the two female protagonists by making it clear that Bingley is still interested in Jane.

Discussion point: Why does Austen revive the Bingley-Jane subplot at this point?

Questions

How does the meeting between Elizabeth and Georgiana go?

Why does Elizabeth stop feeling angry towards Bingley?

What does Elizabeth observe between Bingley and Georgiana?

Why is Elizabeth amazed at Darcy's behaviour towards the Gardiners?

What do the Gardiners realize about Darcy?

What does Elizabeth feel towards Darcy at this point?

You can find the answers for the above questions embedded in the chapter summaries on the **Gradesaver website here.**

GCSE style question: how does Austen create narrative tension in this chapter?

Creative response: write Mrs Gardiner's diary for this chapter, outlining her thoughts about Wickham, Darcy and Elizabeth.

Chapter 45

Questions

How does Georgiana treat Elizabeth and the Gardiners at Pemberley?

How does Caroline Bingley try to embarrass Elizabeth? How does Elizabeth respond?

How and why does Caroline criticize Elizabeth to Georgiana and Darcy? What is Darcy's response?

You can find the answers for the above questions embedded in the chapter summaries on the **Gradesaver website here.**

A Level style question: how does Austen make the conversations between people so intriguing and suspenseful?

Creative response: write Caroline Bingley's diary for this chapter, outlining her feelings towards Darcy, his sister and Elizabeth.

Chapter 46

Extract:

"I am truly glad, dearest Lizzy, that you have been spared something of these distressing scenes; but now, as the first shock is over, shall I own that I long for your return? I am not so selfish, however, as to press for it, if inconvenient. Adieu! I take up my pen again to do what I have just told you I would not; but circumstances are such that I cannot help earnestly begging you all to come here as soon as possible. I know my dear uncle and aunt so well, that I am not afraid of requesting it, though I have still something more to ask of the former. My father is going to London with Colonel Forster instantly, to try to discover her. What he means to do I am sure I know not; but his excessive distress will not allow him to pursue any measure in the best and safest way, and Colonel Forster is obliged to be at Brighton again to-morrow evening. In such an exigence, my uncle's advice and assistance would be everything in the world; he will immediately comprehend what I must feel, and I rely upon his goodness."

Analysis: Just when things were going so well, Austen introduces the drama of Lydia's elopement with Wickham.

Discussion point: Why does Austen introduce the Wickham-Lydia subplot at this point?

Extract:

He readily assured her of his secrecy; again expressed his sorrow for her distress, wished it a happier conclusion than there was at present reason to hope, and leaving his compliments for her relations, with only one serious, parting look, went away.

As he quitted the room, Elizabeth felt how improbable it was that they should ever see each other again on such terms of cordiality as had marked their several meetings in Derbyshire; and as she threw a retrospective glance over the whole of their acquaintance, so full of contradictions and varieties, sighed at the perverseness of those feelings which would now have promoted its continuance, and would formerly have rejoiced in its termination.

Analysis: Here we are presented with the deepening relationship between Elizabeth and Darcy; she is able to share her distress about Lydia with him and feel that she can trust him. She believes that Lydia is 'lost' and, by implication, will become a disgrace to the family, a girl known to have had pre-marital sex. We also enter Elizabeth's mind and see her reflecting upon her relationship with Darcy; 'she threw a retrospective glance over the whole of their acquaintance'.

Discussion point: What does this encounter reveal about the relationship between Darcy and Elizabeth?

Questions

What terrible news does Jane give Elizabeth in two letters?

What does Elizabeth confess to Darcy?

What does Elizabeth realise that this new disgrace will mean for her chances of marrying Darcy? What does this thought then make her realise about her feelings for Darcy?

What does Elizabeth think Wickham's intentions are?

What do the Gardiners decide to do when they hear the news?

You can find the answers for the above questions embedded in the chapter summaries on the **Gradesaver website here.**

GCSE style question: how does Austen create drama and suspense in this chapter?

Creative response: write Elizabeth's diary, exploring her feelings about her family and Darcy.

Chapter 47

Extract:

"My mother is tolerably well, I trust; though her spirits are greatly shaken. She is up stairs and will have great satisfaction in seeing you all. She does not yet leave her dressing-room. Mary and Kitty, thank Heaven, are quite well."

"But you—how are you?" cried Elizabeth. "You look pale. How much you must have gone through!"

> Her sister, however, assured her of her being perfectly well; and their conversation, which had been passing while Mr. and Mrs. Gardiner were engaged with their children, was now put an end to by the approach of the whole party. Jane ran to her uncle and aunt, and welcomed and thanked them both, with alternate smiles and tears.

Analysis: The reunion of the Bennet family is a moving one, considering all that they have gone through and that Lydia has put the name of the whole family at risk.

Discussion point: What do you think of the way Austen presents the Bennet family at this point?

Questions

What does Mr Gardiner believe Wickham's intentions are with Lydia?

How have Lydia, Kitty and Mrs Bennet reacted to the situation when Elizabeth gets back to Longbourn?

Who does Mrs Bennet blame for the situation?

What does Lydia's note to Mrs Forster reveal about Lydia's character and her beliefs regarding Wickham's intentions?

You can find the answers for the above questions embedded in the chapter summaries on the **Gradesaver website here.**

A Level style question: how does Austen create the feeling that there is a great deal at stake in this chapter?

Creative response: write Elizabeth's diary, outlining what she thinks and feels when she returns to Longbourn.

Chapter 48

Extract:

Mr. Gardiner did not write again till he had received an answer from Colonel Forster; and then he had nothing of a pleasant nature to send. It was not known that Wickham had a single relationship with whom he kept up any connection, and it was certain that he had no near one living. His former acquaintances had been numerous; but since he had been in the militia, it did not appear that he was on terms of particular friendship with any of them. There was no one, therefore, who could be pointed out as likely to give any news of him. And in the wretched state of his own finances, there was a very powerful motive for secrecy, in addition to his fear of discovery by Lydia's relations, for it had just transpired that he had left gaming debts behind him to a very considerable amount. Colonel Forster believed that more than a thousand pounds would be necessary to clear his expenses at Brighton. He owed a good deal in town, but his debts of honour were still more formidable. Mr. Gardiner did not attempt to conceal these particulars from the Longbourn family. Jane heard them with horror. "A gamester!" she cried. "This is wholly unexpected. I had not an idea of it."

Mr. Gardiner added in his letter, that they might expect to see their father at home on the following day, which was Saturday. Rendered spiritless by the ill-success of all their endeavours, he had yielded to his brother-in-law's entreaty that he would return to his family, and leave it to him to do whatever occasion might suggest to be advisable for continuing their pursuit. When Mrs. Bennet was told of this, she did not express so much satisfaction as her children expected, considering what her anxiety for his life had been before.

"What, is he coming home, and without poor Lydia?" she cried. "Sure he will not leave London before he has found them. Who is to fight Wickham, and make him marry her, if he comes away?"

As Mrs. Gardiner began to wish to be at home, it was settled that she and the children should go to London, at the same time that Mr. Bennet came from it. The coach, therefore, took them the first stage of their journey, and brought its master back to Longbourn.

Analysis: We learn of the father unable to do anything about the scandal.

Discussion point: What do you think of the way Austen presents the father here?

Questions

What does everyone now think of Wickham's character in Meryton?

What are Mr Gardiner and Mr Bennet doing in London?

What does Mr Collins's letter to Mr Bennet say?

What does Mr Gardiner's next letter reveal about Wickham's debts and why he might be hiding?

Why is Elizabeth worried about the situation?

When Mr Bennet returns, what does he confess to Elizabeth?

You can find the answers for the above questions embedded in the chapter summaries on the **Gradesaver website here.**

GCSE style question: how does Austen increase the narrative tension in this chapter?

Creative response: write Elizabeth's diary, exploring her feelings about Darcy, Wickham, Lydia and Jane.

Chapter 49

Extract:

Elizabeth took the letter from his writing-table, and they went up stairs together. Mary and Kitty were both with Mrs. Bennet: one communication would, therefore, do for all. After a slight preparation for good news, the letter was read aloud. Mrs. Bennet could hardly contain herself. As soon as Jane had read Mr. Gardiner's hope of Lydia's being soon married, her joy burst forth, and every following sentence added to its exuberance. She was now in an irritation as violent from delight, as she had ever been fidgety from alarm and vexation. To know that her daughter would be married was enough. She was disturbed by no fear for her felicity, nor humbled by any remembrance of her misconduct.

Analysis: Here Austen emphasizes the ignorance and stupidity of Mrs Bennet. Mrs Bennet embodies all the things that the central characters have learnt to leave behind: pride and prejudice. She is foolishly proud of Lydia getting married and has not learnt from her previous experiences; 'nor humbled by any remembrance of her misconduct'.

Discussion point: What do you think of the presentation of Mrs Bennet here?

Questions

What does Mr Gardiner's letter say regarding Wickham? On what conditions will he agree to marry Lydia?

What does Mr Bennet assume Mr Gardiner has done regarding Wickham's debts?

What is Mrs Bennet's response to the news?

You can find the answers for the above questions embedded in the chapter summaries on the **Gradesaver website here.**

A Level style question: how does Austen explore the themes of money, property and marriage in the novel?

Creative response: write Mr Bennet's diary for this chapter.

Chapter 50

Extract:

Mr. Bennet and his daughters saw all the advantages of Wickham's removal from the ——shire as clearly as Mr. Gardiner could do. But Mrs. Bennet was not so well pleased with it. Lydia's being settled in the North, just when she had expected most pleasure and pride in her company, for she had by no means given up her plan of their residing in Hertfordshire, was a severe disappointment; and, besides, it was such a pity that Lydia should be taken from a regiment where she was acquainted with everybody, and had so many favourites.

"She is so fond of Mrs. Forster," said she, "it will be quite shocking to send her away! And there are several of the young men, too, that she likes very much. The officers may not be so pleasant in General ——'s regiment."

His daughter's request, for such it might be considered, of being admitted into her family again before she set off for the North, received at first an absolute negative. But Jane and Elizabeth, who agreed in wishing, for the sake of their sister's feelings and consequence, that she should be noticed on her marriage by her parents, urged him so earnestly yet so rationally and so mildly, to receive her and her husband at Longbourn, as soon as they were married, that he was prevailed on to think as they thought, and act as they wished. And their mother had the satisfaction of knowing that she would be able to show her married daughter in the neighbourhood before she was banished to the North.

Analysis: Here we see Elizabeth and Jane almost the roles of heads of the family, persuading their father to accept Lydia and Wickham at Longbourn. They appear to put the needs of their family above the rules of decorum.

Discussion point: How has the Bennet family changed since the beginning of the novel?

Questions

What is Mr Bennet determined to do regarding Mr Gardiner?

What does Mrs Bennet talk about all this time?

What does Mr Bennet say he will not allow? Why is Mrs Bennet so disappointed?

What does Elizabeth believe her prospects with Darcy are likely to be?

What is Wickham planning to do career-wise?

What is the result of Elizabeth and Jane's discussions with Mr Bennet regarding Lydia and Wickham's visit to Longbourn?

You can find the answers for the above questions embedded in the chapter summaries on the **Gradesaver website here.**

GCSE style question: how does Austen present the characters of Mr and Mrs Bennet in this chapter?

Creative response: write Elizabeth's diary for the chapter, discussing her thoughts about Wickham, her parents and Darcy.

Chapter 51

Extract:

"Mr. Darcy!" repeated Elizabeth, in utter amazement.

"Oh, yes!—he was to come there with Wickham, you know. But gracious me! I quite forgot! I ought not to have said a word about it. I promised them so faithfully! What will Wickham say? It was to be such a secret!"

Analysis: Austen introduces a twist in the story of the marriage by letting Lydia accidentally drop in the information that Darcy was there at the marriage.

Discussion point: How does Austen create narrative tension here?

Questions

How do Lydia and Wickham behave when they arrive at Longbourn?

How do Jane and Elizabeth feel about Lydia's behaviour?

Does Lydia show any gratitude towards the Gardiners? Who else attended the wedding? Why do you think Lydia was told to keep his attendance a secret? What is Elizabeth's response? Who does she write to for more details?

You can find the answers for the above questions embedded in the

chapter summaries on the **Gradesaver website here.**

A Level style question: how does Austen present Wickham and Lydia in this chapter?

Creative response: write Elizabeth's diary, talking about response to Lydia's wedding and the mystery guest.

Chapter 52

Extract:

The contents of this letter threw Elizabeth into a flutter of spirits, in which it was difficult to determine whether pleasure or pain bore the greatest share. The vague and unsettled suspicions which uncertainty had produced of what Mr. Darcy might have been doing to forward her sister's match, which she had feared to encourage as an exertion of goodness too great to be probable, and at the same time dreaded to be just, from the pain of obligation, were proved beyond their greatest extent to be true! He had followed them purposely to town, he had taken on himself all the trouble and mortification attendant on such a research; in which supplication had been necessary to a woman whom he must abominate and despise, and where he was reduced to meet, frequently meet, reason with, persuade, and finally bribe, the man whom he always most wished to avoid, and whose very name it was punishment to him to pronounce. He had done all this for a girl whom he could neither regard nor esteem. Her heart did whisper that he had done it for her. But it was a hope shortly checked by other considerations, and she soon felt that even her vanity was insufficient, when required to depend on his affection for her—for a woman who had already refused him—as able to overcome a sentiment so natural as abhorrence against relationship with Wickham. Brother-in-law of Wickham! Every kind of pride must revolt from the connection. He had, to be sure, done much. She was ashamed to think how much. But he had given a reason for his interference, which asked no extraordinary stretch of belief. It was reasonable that he should feel he had been wrong; he had liberality, and he had the means of exercising it; and though she would not place herself as his principal inducement, she could, perhaps, believe that remaining partiality for her might assist his endeavours in a cause where her peace of mind must be materially concerned. It was painful, exceedingly painful, to know that they were under obligations to a person who could never receive a return. They owed the restoration of Lydia, her character, every thing, to him. Oh! how heartily did she grieve over every ungracious sensation she had ever encouraged, every saucy speech she had ever directed towards him.

Analysis: Here Darcy is presented as a hero, a rescuer: "they owed the restoration of Lydia, her character, everything to Mr Darcy."

Discussion point: What do you think of the presentation of
Mr Darcy at this point?

Questions

What does Mrs Gardiner's letter reveal about Darcy? How did he find out
where Wickham was? How did he persuade Wickham to marry Lydia? Why
does Mrs Gardiner think Darcy acted so nobly?

What does Elizabeth think of the letter?

How does Elizabeth behave towards Wickham?

You can find the answers for the above questions embedded in the
chapter summaries on the **Gradesaver website here.**

A Level style question: how does Austen slowly reveal Darcy to be a hero
in this novel?

Creative response: write Elizabeth's diary, outlining her response to Mrs
Gardiner's letter and Wickham.

Chapter 53

Extract:

"It is a delightful thing, to be sure, to have a daughter well married,"
continued her mother, "but at the same time, Mr. Bingley, it is very hard to
have her taken such a way from me. They are gone down to Newcastle, a
place quite northward, it seems, and there they are to stay I do not know
how long. His regiment is there; for I suppose you have heard of his leaving
the ——shire, and of his being gone into the regulars. Thank Heaven! he
has *some* friends, though perhaps not so many as he deserves."

Elizabeth, who knew this to be levelled at Mr. Darcy, was in such misery
of shame, that she could hardly keep her seat. It drew from her, however,
the exertion of speaking, which nothing else had so effectually done before;
and she asked Bingley whether he meant to make any stay in the country at
present. A few weeks, he believed.

"When you have killed all your own birds, Mr. Bingley," said her mother,
"I beg you will come here, and shoot as many as you please on Mr. Bennet's
manor. I am sure he will be vastly happy to oblige you, and will save all the
best of the covies for you."

Elizabeth's misery increased, at such unnecessary, such officious
attention! Were the same fair prospect to arise at present as had flattered
them a year ago, every thing, she was persuaded, would be hastening to the
same vexatious conclusion. At that instant, she felt that years of happiness
could not make Jane or herself amends for moments of such painful
confusion.

"The first wish of my heart," said she to herself, "is never more to be in
company with either of them. Their society can afford no pleasure that will
atone for such wretchedness as this! Let me never see either one or the

other again!"

Yet the misery, for which years of happiness were to offer no compensation, received soon afterwards material relief, from observing how much the beauty of her sister re-kindled the admiration of her former lover. When first he came in, he had spoken to her but little; but every five minutes seemed to be giving her more of his attention. He found her as handsome as she had been last year; as good natured, and as unaffected, though not quite so chatty. Jane was anxious that no difference should be perceived in her at all, and was really persuaded that she talked as much as ever. But her mind was so busily engaged, that she did not always know when she was silent.

When the gentlemen rose to go away, Mrs. Bennet was mindful of her intended civility, and they were invited and engaged to dine at Longbourn in a few days time.

> Analysis: Here we see how Elizabeth has changed in the novel; she is presented as being deeply ashamed by her mother's vulgar pride. She 'dared not lift up her eyes' because she realises just how foolish her mother is to brag about such a 'scandalous' marriage, which Darcy basically forced upon Wickham in order to save the Bennet family from gaining a ruinous reputation.

> Discussion point: Has Elizabeth gained a more snobbish attitude towards her mother now that she is aware that Darcy's eyes are upon her family?

Questions

Where do Lydia and Wickham go? Why is Mrs Bennet sad? What do the rest of the family feel towards Lydia?

Who is returning to Netherfield? What is Jane's response to this news?

What does Elizabeth hope might happen?

How does Mrs Bennet treat Darcy and Bingley when they visit? How does Darcy behave?

You can find the answers for the above questions embedded in the chapter summaries on the **Gradesaver website here.**

A Level style question: how does Austen generate suspense and interest in her description of the visits to Longbourn? For this question, think about a few different visits to Longbourn.

Creative response: write Elizabeth's diary for this chapter, outlining her response to Mrs Bennet's reaction to Darcy, and Darcy's quietness.

Chapter 54

Extract:

She was in hopes that the evening would afford some opportunity of bringing them together; that the whole of the visit would not pass away without enabling them to enter into something more of conversation than the mere ceremonious salutation attending his entrance. Anxious and uneasy, the period which passed in the drawing-room, before the gentlemen came, was wearisome and dull to a degree that almost made her uncivil. She looked forward to their entrance as the point on which all her chance of pleasure for the evening must depend.

"If he does not come to me, *then*," said she, "I shall give him up for ever."

The gentlemen came; and she thought he looked as if he would have answered her hopes; but, alas! the ladies had crowded round the table, where Miss Bennet was making tea, and Elizabeth pouring out the coffee, in so close a confederacy that there was not a single vacancy near her which would admit of a chair. And on the gentlemen's approaching, one of the girls moved closer to her than ever, and said, in a whisper:

"The men shan't come and part us, I am determined. We want none of them; do we?"

Darcy had walked away to another part of the room. She followed him with her eyes, envied everyone to whom he spoke, had scarcely patience enough to help anybody to coffee; and then was enraged against herself for being so silly!

Analysis: How Elizabeth has changed! We see her behaving like a skittish girl with Darcy; 'she followed him with her eyes, envied every one to whom he spoke'. Austen is at pains to present her in a vulnerable state, worried about he might be feeling towards her. Once again, apart from Jane, the Bennet is presented in an unfavourable light, but this time things have changed because, far from being a disinterested, ironic observer of the scene, Elizabeth is profoundly emotionally involved with her family – irritated and embarrassed by them, 'anxious and uneasy' that they might blow her chance of marrying Darcy.

Discussion point: What do you think of the way Elizabeth is presented here?

Questions

Who does Bingley sit next to at dinner? What does Elizabeth think of this?

Why is Elizabeth anxious and annoyed at dinner?

What news does Darcy provide?

Why is Mrs Bennet so pleased with the dinner?

You can find the answers for the above questions embedded in the chapter summaries on the **Gradesaver website here.**

GCSE style question: how does Austen make dinners in the novel so interesting? Think back over the whole novel for this question.

Creative response: write Elizabeth's diary for this question, discussing her feelings towards Darcy.

Chapter 55

Extract:

Jane could have no reserves from Elizabeth, where confidence would give pleasure; and instantly embracing her, acknowledged, with the liveliest emotion, that she was the happiest creature in the world.

"'Tis too much!" she added, "by far too much. I do not deserve it. Oh! why is not everybody as happy?"

Elizabeth's congratulations were given with a sincerity, a warmth, a delight, which words could but poorly express. Every sentence of kindness was a fresh source of happiness to Jane. But she would not allow herself to stay with her sister, or say half that remained to be said for the present.

Analysis: What is fascinating here is the way in which the old customs are blending with the new 'fashion' of love. Bingley meets Mr Bennet to sort out the contractual arrangements of the marriage, but it is clear from the meeting at the hearth that this is a 'love match'; the pair are engaged in 'earnest conversation'. We gain a sense that the marriage is a serious meeting of minds. We have to remember that this is a new mode of being which is being established; Bingley is marrying well 'beneath' himself because he loves Jane. It is not a sensible match in the 'old fashioned' sense; Jane has now money or status. However, Austen shows that we are living in different times now; 'love' has its place amidst the hierarchy. It is a justifiable reason for getting married. And yet, it is new; there are no really established customs attached to it. When the lovers see Elizabeth they are deeply embarrassed, and so is Elizabeth. There is real tension because no one really knows how to behave in this brave new world. Jane and Bingley, having being rapt in conversation, now 'hastily' turn around. Their situation was 'awkward' because there are no set rules for decorous behaviour in this situation – and even less for Elizabeth.

We gain an even greater sense that we are entering a new era by the way that Elizabeth congratulates her sister on the engagement. Her congratulations are 'given with a sincerity, a warmth, a delight, which words could but poorly express'. Elizabeth and Jane are the new generation who are forging a new language of the emotions; a world where 'sincerity' and authentic conduct are paramount.

Discussion point: How does Austen create tension in this scene?

Questions

What does Mrs Bennet try and do with Bingley when he visits? What does she manage to do with Bingley and Jane on his second visit, the next morning?

What does Elizabeth think is happening between Jane and Bingley when she walks into the drawing room?

What news does Jane give when Bingley leaves the drawing room?

What happens when Bingley returns? What is the news?

You can find the answers for the above questions embedded in the chapter summaries on the **Gradesaver website here.**

A Level style question: how does Austen make proposals in the novel so exciting and momentous? Think back over the whole novel.

Creative response: write Jane's diary for this chapter, discussing her feelings for Bingley.

Chapter 56

One morning, about a week after Bingley's engagement with Jane had been formed, as he and the females of the family were sitting together in the dining-room, their attention was suddenly drawn to the window, by the sound of a carriage; and they perceived a chaise and four driving up the lawn. It was too early in the morning for visitors, and besides, the equipage did not answer to that of any of their neighbours. The horses were post; and neither the carriage, nor the livery of the servant who preceded it, were familiar to them. As it was certain, however, that somebody was coming, Bingley instantly prevailed on Miss Bennet to avoid the confinement of such an intrusion, and walk away with him into the shrubbery. They both set off, and the conjectures of the remaining three continued, though with little satisfaction, till the door was thrown open and their visitor entered. It was Lady Catherine de Bourgh.

They were of course all intending to be surprised; but their astonishment was beyond their expectation; and on the part of Mrs. Bennet and Kitty, though she was perfectly unknown to them, even inferior to what Elizabeth felt.

She entered the room with an air more than usually ungracious, made no other reply to Elizabeth's salutation than a slight inclination of the head, and sat down without saying a word. Elizabeth had mentioned her name to her mother on her ladyship's entrance, though no request of introduction had been made.

Analysis: Lady Catherine de Bourgh is presented as highly presumptuous and rude here, a huge contrast to behaviour of the two sisters.

Discussion point: Why does Austen orchestrate Lady Catherine's entrance in this way?

Extract:

"I will not be interrupted. Hear me in silence. My daughter and my nephew are formed for each other. They are descended, on the maternal side, from the same noble line; and, on the father's, from respectable, honourable, and ancient—though untitled—families. Their fortune on both sides is splendid. They are destined for each other by the voice of every member of their respective houses; and what is to divide them? The upstart pretensions of a young woman without family, connections, or fortune. Is this to be endured! But it must not, shall not be. If you were sensible of your own good, you would not wish to quit the sphere in which you have been brought up."

"In marrying your nephew, I should not consider myself as quitting that sphere. He is a gentleman; I am a gentleman's daughter; so far we are equal."

"True. You *are* a gentleman's daughter. But who was your mother? Who are your uncles and aunts? Do not imagine me ignorant of their condition."

"Whatever my connections may be," said Elizabeth, "if your nephew does not object to them, they can be nothing to *you*."

"Tell me once for all, are you engaged to him?"

Though Elizabeth would not, for the mere purpose of obliging Lady Catherine, have answered this question, she could not but say, after a moment's deliberation:

"I am not."

Lady Catherine seemed pleased.

"And will you promise me, never to enter into such an engagement?"

"I will make no promise of the kind."

Analysis: Austen creates this extremely tense but comic scene by engineering a clash between the old ways and the new. Lady Catherine represents a 'dying' order in the novel. Her rigid belief in 'honour, decorum, prudence' have been conquered by Elizabeth's adherence to being 'sincere, kind, warm'. These new values descend and over-rule the ones of the aristocracy; if someone has them then they are entitled to ignore the imperative of 'knowing one's place' of being honourable and marrying someone from one's own class. Austen creates real tension because Lady Catherine tries to bully Elizabeth into rejecting Darcy again. But her 'pride' will not defeat Elizabeth.

Discussion point: Why does Austen write such a dramatic scene near the end of the novel?

Questions

Who visits Longbourn the next day? Who does she want to speak to in private and why? What news has this person heard about? What questions does she ask Elizabeth? What is Elizabeth's response? What does she forbid Elizabeth to do? What is Elizabeth's response?

You can find the answers for the above questions embedded in the chapter summaries on the **Gradesaver website here.**

GCSE style question: how does Austen present Lady Catherine in this novel?

Creative response: write Elizabeth's diary for this chapter, outlining her feelings about Lady Catherine.

Chapter 57

Questions

Why does the conversation with Lady Catherine upset Elizabeth?

Why does Mr Bennet want to speak to Elizabeth? What does Mr Collins's letter reveal and advise?

What is Mr Bennet's response to the letter?

You can find the answers for the above questions embedded in the chapter summaries on the **Gradesaver website here.**

A Level style question: who are the snobbish people in the novel? How is their snobbery revealed? Think back over the whole novel.

Creative response: write Elizabeth's diary, exploring her feelings about Mr Collins's letter.

Chapter 58

Extract

"On the evening before my going to London," said he, "I made a confession to him, which I believe I ought to have made long ago. I told him of all that had occurred to make my former interference in his affairs absurd and impertinent. His surprise was great. He had never had the slightest suspicion. I told him, moreover, that I believed myself mistaken in supposing, as I had done, that your sister was indifferent to him; and as I could easily perceive that his attachment to her was unabated, I felt no doubt of their happiness together."

Elizabeth could not help smiling at his easy manner of directing his friend.

"Did you speak from your own observation," said she, "when you told him that my sister loved him, or merely from my information last spring?"

"From the former. I had narrowly observed her during the two visits which I had lately made here; and I was convinced of her affection."

"And your assurance of it, I suppose, carried immediate conviction to him."

"It did. Bingley is most unaffectedly modest. His diffidence had prevented his depending on his own judgment in so anxious a case, but his reliance on mine made every thing easy. I was obliged to confess one thing, which for a time, and not unjustly, offended him. I could not allow myself to conceal that your sister had been in town three months last winter, that I had known it, and purposely kept it from him. He was angry. But his anger, I am persuaded, lasted no longer than he remained in any doubt of your sister's sentiments. He has heartily forgiven me now."

Elizabeth longed to observe that Mr. Bingley had been a most delightful friend; so easily guided that his worth was invaluable; but she checked herself. She remembered that he had yet to learn to be laughed at, and it was rather too early to begin. In anticipating the happiness of Bingley, which of course was to be inferior only to his own, he continued the conversation till they reached the house. In the hall they parted.

Analysis: The second proposal scene is in marked contrast to the first; here we see Darcy without his pride, and Elizabeth without her prejudice. We also see her beginning to forge a new morality. When she says, *"my conduct, my manners, my expressions during the whole of it- is now, and has been many months, inexpressibly painful to me"* we realise that Elizabeth has not rejected all the old notions of 'conducting' oneself properly. Far from it, she has rather injected new life into the concept of 'manners'; she believes that manners should informed by unprejudiced mind, which has authentic, sincere motivations.

Discussion point: How does this proposal scene contrast with the first proposal scene with Darcy?

Questions

Who goes for a walk together and why? List all the people.

What does Elizabeth thank Darcy for?

What does Darcy tell her?

What does Darcy ask her about her feelings?

Why does Darcy say he had the courage to propose to her again?

What do Darcy and Elizabeth say about the first difficult proposal?

What de Darcy and Elizabeth both say they have come to realise about themselves? What do they say their mistakes were?

You can find the answers for the above questions embedded in the chapter summaries on the **Gradesaver website here.**

A Level style question: how does Austen make this second proposal so different from the first? Why is getting engaged never actually discussed?

Creative response: write Darcy's diary for this scene, exploring his feelings and thoughts about Elizabeth.

Chapter 59

Extract:

At night she opened her heart to Jane. Though suspicion was very far from Miss Bennet's general habits, she was absolutely incredulous here.

"You are joking, Lizzy. This cannot be!—engaged to Mr. Darcy! No, no, you shall not deceive me. I know it to be impossible."

"This is a wretched beginning indeed! My sole dependence was on you; and I am sure nobody else will believe me, if you do not. Yet, indeed, I am in earnest. I speak nothing but the truth. He still loves me, and we are engaged."

Jane looked at her doubtingly. "Oh, Lizzy! it cannot be. I know how much you dislike him."

"You know nothing of the matter. *That* is all to be forgot. Perhaps I did not always love him so well as I do now. But in such cases as these, a good memory is unpardonable. This is the last time I shall ever remember it myself."

Miss Bennet still looked all amazement. Elizabeth again, and more seriously assured her of its truth.

"Good Heaven! can it be really so! Yet now I must believe you," cried Jane. "My dear, dear Lizzy, I would—I do congratulate you—but are you certain? forgive the question—are you quite certain that you can be happy with him?"

"There can be no doubt of that. It is settled between us already, that we are to be the happiest couple in the world. But are you pleased, Jane? Shall you like to have such a brother?"

"Very, very much. Nothing could give either Bingley or myself more delight. But we considered it, we talked of it as impossible. And do you really love him quite well enough? Oh, Lizzy! do anything rather than marry without affection. Are you quite sure that you feel what you ought to do?"

"Oh, yes! You will only think I feel *more* than I ought to do, when I tell you all."

"What do you mean?"

"Why, I must confess that I love him better than I do Bingley. I am afraid you will be angry."

"My dearest sister, now *be* serious. I want to talk very seriously. Let me know every thing that I am to know, without delay. Will you tell me how long you have loved him?"

"It has been coming on so gradually, that I hardly know when it began. But I believe I must date it from my first seeing his beautiful grounds at Pemberley."

Analysis: Here we see the two sisters discuss the vital issue; *'do anything rather than marry without affection'*. The word 'affection' is important because it is less strident than the abstract noun 'love' but carries with it similar connotations; at the heart of any good marriage is genuine feeling. However, it does also suggest that the emotions in a marriage should be informed by notions of proper conduct. Elizabeth's confession that she first fell in love with Darcy when she saw Pemberley further endorses this point; the grounds revealed nature in a balanced, civilised and sincere way.

Discussion point: Why did Elizabeth first start falling in love with Darcy when she saw Pemberley? What point is Austen trying to make here? That Elizabeth only loves Darcy for his property?

Extract:

"This is an evening of wonders, indeed! And so, Darcy did every thing; made up the match, gave the money, paid the fellow's debts, and got him his commission! So much the better. It will save me a world of trouble and economy. Had it been your uncle's doing, I must and *would* have paid him; but these violent young lovers carry every thing their own way. I shall offer to pay him to-morrow; he will rant and storm about his love for you, and there will be an end of the matter."

Analysis: Here, we gain an insight into the complexity of Elizabeth's relationship with her father. Although he has given Darcy's consent to marry Lizzy, we see him full of doubts. He questions her, saying: *"what are you doing? are you out of your senses, to be accepting this man? Have not you always hated him?"* We gain a sense that Mr Bennet is very wary of his favourite daughter marrying 'badly'. However, as ever with Mr Bennet, we can never be sure if this isn't typical of his contrarian style; he rarely, if ever, makes life easy for his family. We also have a sense that he will be lonely without Elizabeth; she is one intellectual equal in the family. He will be losing a life-time companion. Elizabeth's final confession that she loves him with tears in her eyes is moving because she has been so restrained until this moment.

Discussion point: How does Austen create tension in this scene?

Questions

What does Elizabeth tell Jane? What is Jane's response?
How does Darcy annoy Mrs Bennet?
What does Elizabeth realise Bingley knows?
What is Mr Bennet's response to Darcy's proposal? What does Elizabeth

reassure him of?

What persuades Mrs Bennet to like Mr Darcy?

You can find the answers for the above questions embedded in the chapter summaries on the **Gradesaver website here.**

GCSE style question: how does Austen present Elizabeth's relationship with her parents at the end of the novel?

Creative response: write Mr Bennet's diary for this chapter, outlining his thoughts and feelings about Darcy, Elizabeth and his daughters generally.

Chapter 60

Questions

What does Elizabeth want to know from Darcy?

Who do Darcy and Elizabeth write to and why? What responses do they get and why?

GCSE style question: how does Austen portray Elizabeth and Darcy's relationship now that they are together?

Creative response: write Elizabeth's diary for this chapter, outlining her thoughts about the letters that she and other people have written.

Chapter 61

Extract:

Lady Catherine was extremely indignant on the marriage of her nephew; and as she gave way to all the genuine frankness of her character in her reply to the letter which announced its arrangement, she sent him language so very abusive, especially of Elizabeth, that for some time all intercourse was at an end. But at length, by Elizabeth's persuasion, he was prevailed on to overlook the offence, and seek a reconciliation; and, after a little further resistance on the part of his aunt, her resentment gave way, either to her affection for him, or her curiosity to see how his wife conducted herself; and she condescended to wait on them at Pemberley, in spite of that pollution which its woods had received, not merely from the presence of such a mistress, but the visits of her uncle and aunt from the city.

With the Gardiners, they were always on the most intimate terms. Darcy, as well as Elizabeth, really loved them; and they were both ever sensible of the warmest gratitude towards the persons who, by bringing her into Derbyshire, had been the means of uniting them.

Analysis: Austen's resolution to the novel is full of irony. We see Mrs Bennet continue in her deluded state, visiting her daughters with 'delighted pride' exhibiting the very emotion that put a block on both marriages. Mr Bennet is presented as somewhat lost; but perhaps being a bit troubling because he visits when least expected. A reconciliation of sorts happens between Lady Catherine and the Darcys, but it is clearly difficult and edgy. Austen finally turns her attention to the Gardiners, who play a small but crucial role in the novel, by bringing Elizabeth into contact with Pemberley.

Discussion point: To what extent is this a successful resolution to the novel?

Questions

How do the following people react to the news of Darcy's marriage: Georgiana, Lady Catherine, Mr Collins, Charlotte Lucas, and Mrs Bennet.

How do the couples (Bingley/Jane; Darcy/Elizabeth) enjoy marriage? What happens to them? What happens to the other daughters? How and why does Caroline Bingley change in her attitude towards the marriage?

What happens to Darcy's relationship with Lady Catherine?

Why do Darcy and Elizabeth remain on friendly terms with the Gardiners?

You can find the answers for the above questions embedded in the chapter summaries on the **Gradesaver website here.**

A Level style question: how successful is this resolution to the novel?

Creative response: write your final entry of Elizabeth's diary, outlining how she feels about married life.

Speaking and Listening Exercises

Work in a group and devise a **chatshow** based on the novel. Make sure that you have an interviewer (chat-show host) who questions the main characters in the novel about their thoughts and feelings regarding what has happened to them. The aim is that students need to show that they understand the storyline and characters by talking in role about the events in the novel.

You could put Wickham on **trial** for his defaulting on his debts. Set things up so that you have a prosecuting lawyer who is accusing Wickham of deliberately deceiving the people he owes money. Have a defence lawyer who argues that there is evidence that Wickham should be treated leniently. Call witnesses for the prosecution and defence who are characters from the novel or the author. You could have Elizabeth/Jane/Darcy being called for the prosecution, claiming Wickham is deliberately deceitful, and Lydia, Mrs Bennet, and possibly Mrs Gardiner and Miss King defending him. Use the trial to explore different views on the novel. Then possibly write it up as a script or review what you have learnt from doing it.

Put the main characters in **therapy**. Have them visit a therapist to discuss their problems with the therapist. You could do this so that they go into therapy at various stages during the novel, i.e. Darcy/Elizabeth go into therapy after the disastrous first proposal. Write a review of what you have learnt from doing this afterwards.

Work in a group and devise a **radio drama** of the major parts of the novel. Different groups could work on different sections of the book; e.g. the opening when Bingley/Darcy come to Netherfield, Mr Collins' arrival at Longbourn, the first proposal scene, the arrival of Wickham, the second proposal scene and the marriages. Make the drama short and punchy. This exercise will help you get to know the text in much more depth: the editing of the novel will help you summarise key points.

How to write top grade essays on the novel

In order to write a good essay about *Pride and Prejudice*, you need to understand it. You will need to know what the difficult vocabulary means and be aware of how the text is the product of the world it comes from: late eighteenth century/early nineteenth century England. You will also need to be aware of what the examiners for your particular question are looking for. For GCSE, it appears that most questions are, at the time of writing this guide, "extract based" (**see p. 15 of this PDF of a mock exam issued by AQA here**); you will be given a small extract and asked to consider how the author builds suspense or drama in the extract, or presents the characters in a particular way. In order to achieve highly, you will need to answer the question carefully and not simply re-tell the extract; this is something that I have seen many good students do. The A Level questions on *Pride and Prejudice* are much more like the ones posed in the **essay question section** of this study guide. Sometimes, you might be asked to compare the novel with other literary texts, depending upon the nature of the task and/or exam board. For A Level, you need to be aware of other literary critics' views on the novel.

You should consider a few key questions:

For extract questions, consider how has the author **built up** to this particular moment. Think carefully about what the reader already knows before they have read the extract. You will need to know the story well in order to do this.

What literary devices does the author use to make the passage interesting or to reveal a particular character in a certain light? Think very carefully about the author's use of language: Austen's use of descriptions to create a certain atmosphere or paint a sketch of a character/event; her use of dialogue to reveal character and create drama/tension; her use of imagery (metaphors/similes/personification). You will need to pack your essay full of the relevant terminology if you want to aim for higher marks as it appears many mark schemes as a key requirement.

You need to be aware of a number of different interpretations of the novel. The weblinks below should help you with this.

Finally, you need to provide evidence and analysis to back up your points. As a cornerstone of your essay writing technique, you should be aware of the **PEEL** method of analysing texts: making a Point, providing Evidence, Explaining how your evidence endorses your point, and Linking to a new point.

Writing about the story/narrative

I would strongly advise you to read my section on the **structure and themes of the novel here**. There are many, many things to say about the story of the book, but you should think about your own personal response as well: what did you find the most engaging part of the novel and why? Look back over the notes you have made while you read the novel and use them to shape an original response. You need to avoid just re-telling the story, which is very easy to do in high pressure piece of work and you're not thinking straight!

Writing about the characterisations

There are many websites which can help you with writing about the characters in the novel, including the **Cliffnotes website here**. What most of them don't say is a very important thing I've already mentioned; Austen's characters are NOT real people, they are literary creations and we become interested in them because of their similarities and differences. A central technique of Austen's is to make the reader think about how and why characters are similar and difference; we are constantly being invited to compare and contrast characters in our minds. This is a central way that Austen generates suspense and drama in the novel; although Elizabeth is Jane's sister, she is very different from her. Where Jane is quite quiet and compliant, Elizabeth is feisty and argumentative. Where Darcy is active and rude at the beginning of the novel, his friend Bingley is passive and polite; the effect of this at the beginning of the novel is to make the reader possibly dislike Darcy and prefer Bingley, but as the novel progresses I think the reader warms more to Darcy because he is much more dynamic. Where Mrs Bennet is ignorant and pushy, Mr Bennet is knowledgeable and retiring; this striking contrast makes Mrs Bennet even more nightmarish and funny because her husband is so different.

Task

Look at some character studies online, such as the Cliffnotes one, and devise a chart or visual organiser which illustrates the similarities and differences between the characters, exploring the effect that these similarities and differences have upon the reader.

Writing about the settings

Jane Austen is an interesting writer because unlike many novelists she does not spend much time describing the physical details of her settings, but they are very important. There is Longbourn where the Bennets live; Netherfield Park where the Bingleys reside; Rosings where Lady Catherine has her aristocratic residence; and, possibly most famously, the fabulous Pemberley, the home of the Darcys.

Task

Look carefully at the use of settings in the novel; what purpose do they serve in the novel? Why does Austen set particular scenes in particular settings? The best website to start with is the Pemberley website when examining settings, with links to all the relevant parts of the text:
http://www.pemberley.com/janeinfo/ppjalmap.html

Comedy

As I have already said, a central technique of Austen's is to make the reader laugh or smile; the novel is supposed to be comic! Once you begin to appreciate the humour and understand how Austen generates comedic scenes and characters, you will be in a better place to analyse the novel. A central technique which creates humour is her use of irony in many different forms. At times, Austen is gently ironic with the narrator not quite meaning what she is saying; the use of the third person voice (he/she) is important here. It is a question of tone and approach and needs to explored in a subtle, nuanced fashion.

I found these websites were the clearest explanations of the different types of irony:
http://maenglishnotespk.blogspot.co.uk/2014/06/irony-in-pride-and-prejudice.html
https://beamingnotes.com/2013/06/24/irony-in-pride-and-prejudice/

Austen also uses social satire to enhance the comedy; satire is mocking people for a particular purpose. Austen usually deploys satire to expose snobbery (Lady Catherine), hypocrisy (Darcy) or sycophancy (Mr Collins). There is a useful website here on this:
http://sunnyenglishliterature.blogspot.co.uk/2011/05/use-of-satire-in-pride-and-prejudice.html

Task

Look back over the novel, and work out what the humorous parts of the novel are and why they are funny. Devise a visual organiser which charts the comedic moments so that you can see clearly on one page where the comic moments occur, and think about the effect they have upon the reader.

Use of language

Above all, you need to explore the effects of Austen's language upon the reader; exploring what the language makes the reader think, feel and see.

These websites contain some incisive analysis on the use of language:

https://www.teachingenglish.org.uk/article/pride-prejudice-art-conversation

http://neboliterature.mrkdevelopment.com.au/novel/pride-and-prejudice/Pride-and-Prejudice-Language.html

Task

Devise a chart/visual organiser/notes on the different types of language Austen uses in the novel, providing quotes and examples for the following types of language:

Descriptive language: language which describes people, places and situations

Imagery: language which makes comparisons

Important dialogue: important quotes that people say that make the plot move on.

Useful links

The Shmoop section on literary devices is useful but don't copy it blindly. Read it through and look at the other sites such as Sparknotes/Cliffnotes etc, and come to your own judgements about you think are the important points:

http://www.shmoop.com/pride-and-prejudice/literary-devices.html

Personally, I think the British Library contains the best resources for Austen on the web, with a wealth of original manuscripts, reviews and videos to look at. A good place to start is here, with an early review of the novel:

http://www.bl.uk/collection-items/1813-review-of-pride-and-prejudice

I thought the Pemberley website was excellent for helping you find a particular theme or character very quickly within the text; this will really help you write an original essay on the book. Scroll through the webpage and you'll see what I mean:

http://www.pemberley.com/janeinfo/pridprej.html

The Literature Network has a good page on *Pride and Prejudice*, which contains links to quizzes and criticism:

http://www.online-literature.com/austen/prideprejudice/

The following academic essay is aimed at university students and above, but it is clearly written and argues that the novel is really about the nature of criticism: people being criticized and their responses to being criticized. You can find it here:

http://www.jasna.org/persuasions/printed/number22/gilman.pdf

Some top modern day critics and writers comment on the novel on its

200th anniversary:
http://www.theguardian.com/books/2013/jan/26/pride-prejudice-200th-anniversary

This academic essay is very useful at summarizing the different feminist interpretations of Jane Austen's work; it is about all her work, but most of the points apply to *Pride and Prejudice*:
http://www.jasna.org/persuasions/printed/number14/marshall.pdf

This webpage is quite good at discussing what other famous writers thought of Austen's work:
http://flavorwire.com/408384/jane-austens-most-famous-trolls-critics-and-doubters

Possible essay titles

To what extent is *Pride and Prejudice* a novel about marriage?

"*Pride and Prejudice* is a novel which presents women as oppressed by male society". To what extent do you agree with this statement?

"Jane Austen maintains narrative tension in the novel by constantly making us when and how the main characters (Elizabeth/Darcy, Bingley/Jane) will get married, but we never doubt they will." To what extent do you agree with this statement?

"*Pride and Prejudice* is primarily a romantic comedy and is not serious exploration of humanity's dark side." To what extent do you agree with this statement?

"*Pride and Prejudice* is an inherently conservative novel which celebrates the upper classes more than it condemns them." To what extent do you agree with this statement?

Glossary

Augustan literature is a style of English literature produced during the early 18th century in which the novel first developed, with the characteristics of rationality and balance and harmony being paramount in helping shaping the narratives and verse of the era.

Authorial An adjective meaning 'belonging to the author or writer'

Autobiography A personal account of the author's own life, with the events usually relayed in the order in which they happened

Bluebeard A terrifying figure in a fairytale who locked up and killed his wives

Byronic Like Lord Byron; i.e. romantic, passionate, immoral, sexually promiscuous in some contexts

Contexts The worlds from which a text is created and emerges; the social, biographical and literary background to a text

Dynamic (n) Movement

Elliptical Concise, perhaps surprising

Genre Type of text, e.g. horror, sci-fi, Gothic

Gothic An adjective describing narratives which are full of supernatural happenings and extreme emotions, involving damsels in distress in haunted castles

Hero / heroine The main character (male / female) in a narrative, who exhibits truly fine qualities

Homophone A word which sounds the same as another but is spelt differently, e.g. 'there, their, they're'

Imagery All the poetic devices in a text, in particular the visual images created for the reader's mind to feed on and the comparisons that make a reader think and reflect upon an issue

Irony A statement that, when taken in context, may actually mean the opposite of what is written literally; the use of words expressing something other than their literal intention;

Melodrama A story with extreme emotional events and characters, e.g. suicides, threats, blackmail, mad wives, lustful husbands

Novel A made-up, extended story

Polymath A person of great learning in several fields of study. A person of great learning in several fields of study.

Protagonist The main character

Radical Extreme (politically or otherwise)

Rationality the quality of being consistent with or based on logic

Realism In literature, a movement which aimed to simulate 'reality' in fiction

Satire – A work which mocks or ridicules (usually humorously) an individual or a prevailing trend (adj. satirical)

Sensibility / Sensibilities A characteristic of people who think deeply and responsively about issues

Subversive Troublesome, rebellious, seeking to overthrow a current system

Symbolic Representative of a particular issue or message, e.g. Bertha Mason's cutting of the bridal dress is symbolic of Rochester's betrayal of her

Theme An important idea in a text

Tone An atmosphere conveyed in the writing

NB: You can find a list of the difficult words as they appear in the novel here:

https://myvocabulary.com/word-list/novels/pride-and-prejudice-vocabulary/

About the Author

Francis Gilbert is a Lecturer in Education at Goldsmiths, University of London teaching on the PGCE Secondary English programme and the MA in Children's Literature with Professor Michael Rosen. Previously, he worked for a quarter of a century in various English state schools teaching English and Media Studies to 11-18 year olds. He has also moonlighted as a journalist, novelist and social commentator both in the UK and international media. He is the author of 'Teacher On The Run', 'Yob Nation', 'Parent Power', 'Working The System -- How To Get The Very Best State Education for Your Child', and a novel about school, 'The Last Day Of Term'. His first book, 'I'm A Teacher, Get Me Out Of Here' was a big hit, becoming a bestseller and being serialised on Radio 4. In his role as an English teacher, he has taught many classic texts over the years and has developed a great many resources to assist readers with understanding, appreciating and responding to them both analytically and creatively. This led him to set up his own small publishing company FGI Publishing (fgipublishing.com) which has published his study guides as well as a number of books by other authors, including Roger Titcombe's 'Learning Matters'.

He is the co-founder, with Melissa Benn and Fiona Millar, of The Local Schools Network, **www.localschoolsnetwork.org.uk**, a blog that celebrates non-selective state schools, and also has his own website, **www.francisgilbert.co.uk** and a Mumsnet blog, **www.talesbehindtheclassroomdoor.co.uk**.

He has appeared numerous times on radio and TV, including Newsnight, the Today Programme, Woman's Hour and the Russell Brand Show. In June 2015, he was awarded a PhD in Creative Writing and Education by the University of London.

CPSIA information can be obtained
at www.ICGtesting.com
Printed in the USA
LVHW040401300523
748366LV00005B/308